POSITIVE INTERACTION SKILLS

ROBIN DYNES

POSITIVE INTERACTION SKILLS

A Group Therapy Manual

Speechmark

Speechmark Publishing Ltd · Telford Road · Bicester · Oxon OX26 4LQ · UK

First published in 2004 by
Speechmark Publishing Ltd, Telford Road, Bicester, Oxon OX26 4LQ, UK
www.speechmark.net

© Robin Dynes, 2004

All rights reserved. The whole of this work, including all text and illustrations, is protected by copyright. No part of it may be copied, altered, adapted or otherwise exploited in any way without express prior permission, unless it is in accordance with the provisions of the Copyright Designs and Patents Act 1988 or in order to photocopy or make duplicating masters of those pages so indicated, without alteration and including copyright notices, for the express purposes of instruction and examination. No parts of this work may otherwise be loaded, stored, manipulated, reproduced, or transmitted in any form or by any means, electronic or mechanical, including photocopying and recording, or by any information, storage and retrieval system without prior written permission from the publisher, on behalf of the copyright owner.

002-5101/Printed in the United Kingdom/1010

British Library Cataloguing in Publication Data
Dynes, Robin
  Positive interaction skills : a group therapy manual
  1. Group facilitation 2. Interpersonal communication – Study and teaching
  I. Title
  302.3'4'071

ISBN 0 86388 360 5

Contents

List of handouts		vi
Introduction		1
Part 1: Preparing to run an interaction skills group		7
Introduction		9
Organising the group		11
Guidelines for success		18
Strategies to overcome common problems		22
Part 2: Positive interaction skills sessions		31
1	Introducing positive interaction skills	33
2	Exploring social perception	45
3	Recognising influences on interactaction	59
4	Developing support networks	73
5	Understanding body language	85
6	Making conversation	95
7	Learning to listen	107
8	Starting, sustaining and ending friendships	119
9	Establishing and keeping close relationships	129
10	Appreciating other points of view	141
11	Creating trust and learning to self-disclose	153
12	Resolving conflict in relationships	165
13	Being assertive and handling criticism	177
14	Overcoming shyness and loneliness	193
15	Building confidence and self-esteem	209
16	Managing emotions	221
17	Improving self-management skills	233
18	Ending the group	247
Appendix 1		255

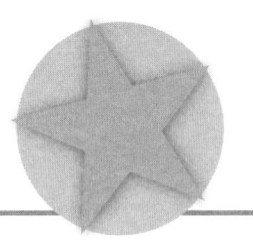

List of handouts

Session 1

1	What is on offer?	43
2	Skills evaluation	44

Session 2

1	What are communities?	52
2	Benefits of belonging to communities	53
3	Self-esteem and communities	54
4	Communities I belong to – example	56
5	Communities I belong to	57

Session 3

1	Things you learn from people around you	65
2	Influences of family and friends	66
3	Influences on personal development	67
4	Messages and effects from the case studies	69
5	My personal development	70
6	Behaviour message and development awareness chart	71

Session 4

1	What is a support network?	79
2	Example support network chart	80
3	Personal support network chart	81
4	Giving in return	82
5	Support network changes	83

Session 5

1	Body language check	94

Session 6

1	Having something to say	101
2	Thinking about making a conversation	102
3	Learning from experience	103
4	Conversation checklist	105

Session 7

1	Defining 'active listening'	113
2	Active listening techniques	114
3	Active listening awareness checklist	116
4	Active listening checklist	117

Session 8

1	What are friends?	124
2	Starting friendships	125
3	Sustaining friendships	126
4	When friendships end	127
5	Homework	128

Session 9

1	Why have close relationships?	135
2	Making it happen	136
3	What I want	137
4	Managing changes	138
5	Moving on	139
6	Improving a relationship	140

Session 10

1	Why bother?	147
2	Other viewpoint situations	148
3	Learning to see	149
4	Negotiating a compromise	150
5	Looking at other points of view	151

Session 11

1	Boundaries situation	161
2	Different level of trust	162
3	How self-disclosure happens	163
4	Trust and disclosure checklist	164

Session 12

1	Causes of conflict	170
2	The framework	171
3	The framework – case study	173
4	Responses to conflict	174
5	Conflict resolution skills checklist	175

Session 13

1	Three types of behaviour	184
2	Identifying behaviours	187
3	Feelings	189
4	Dealing with criticism	191
5	Assertiveness and handling criticism checklist	192

Session 14

1	Shyness reaction chart	200
2	Strategies for coping with shyness	201
3	Shyness action chart	204
4	Overcoming loneliness suggestions	205
5	Identifying barriers	206
6	Overcoming barriers chart	207

Session 15

1	Defining confidence and self-esteem	214
2	Likes and dislikes	215
3	Messages	216
4	Building confidence and self-esteem	217
5	Confidence and self-esteem checklist	220

Session 16

1	Reaction chain	226
2	Emotional reaction chains experienced	227
3	Strategies for managing feelings	228
4	Coping strategies for emotional reaction chains	231
5	Managing emotions checklist	232

Session 17

1	Strategies	239
2	Example stress reaction chart and action plan	240
3	Stress reaction chart and action plan	242
4	Creating the right impression	244
5	Creating the right impression exercise	245
6	Self-management checklist	246

Session 18

1	A positive outlook	251
2	Skills evaluation checklist	252
3	Maintaining and developing skills	253
4	Action plan	254

Introduction

The aim of this book is to provide group leaders with a flexible programme to teach interaction skills that can be adapted to a wide variety of groups, situations and needs. It is particularly useful for groups of adults who have very few or no formal qualifications.

The development of interaction skills is now a well-recognised need in the treatment of depression and schizophrenia, and for other people who become socially isolated. It is also necessary that the skills are taught in schools to young people and to people with learning disabilities.

This book will be useful to occupational therapists, nursing staff, teachers, probation officers, counsellors, youth leaders, social workers, care staff, community psychiatric nurses, probation officers or anyone wanting to run an interaction skills programme.

Who can benefit from the positive interaction programme?

The programme should benefit anyone who lacks adequate skills or who has difficulty interacting with other people at home, socially or at work. They may lack the skills to form and maintain relationships, to develop social networks or they may simply want to improve their skills. Some people may never have acquired adequate interaction skills or may have become socially isolated; they may have an impoverished quality of life and need to regain their abilities. For example, individuals may have difficulty starting a conversation, making friends or being assertive; they may lack listening skills or the ability to resolve conflict in relationships when it arises.

Why work on interaction skills?

Effective interaction skills are required in all relationships. They support individuals' sense of self-esteem and enable them to function, to achieve their ambitions and improve their quality of life. They may want to expand their social network and get on better with people at home or at work. They may lack the confidence or self-esteem necessary to do this. Improved interaction skills will enable individuals to communicate their feelings, thoughts and needs to others. The programme will also teach them how to respond better to other people's feelings, thoughts and needs. They will be able to get what they want more often and will be able to avoid doing things they do not want to do. It will help them to become more independent and achieve goals of their own choice.

Why learn in a group?

Groups provide an ideal setting for promoting interaction skills. Natural interactions are accommodated, along with an opportunity to give and receive support, and to form new relationships within a community setting. Each person becomes aware that he or she is not the only person with interaction difficulties and feels less isolated and alone.

As the group progresses, members are able to see themselves providing support, helping others communicate and receiving support themselves. This helps to promote trust and to build a better self-image. Members will also be encouraged to negotiate options and to make choices as part of a social group. The dynamics within the group provide a natural setting for interaction skills to be developed.

Using the book

The book is divided into two parts:

Part 1: Preparing to run a positive interaction skills group

This section provides some basic issues to consider before beginning an interaction skills group. It will be useful to read through Part 1 whether you are an experienced or an inexperienced group leader. This material includes organising the group, selecting group members and dealing with common problems.

Part 2: Positive interaction skills sessions

The aim of Part 2 is to provide group leaders with enough information to enable them to facilitate a group and discuss its application. The two-hour sessions are designed to be used flexibly, and group leaders should adapt the materials to meet the needs of particular groups and individual group members. For example, if a two-hour session proves too long for a particular group's concentration, take each session over two weeks in one-hour slots. Session plans and activities should be treated as suggestions and you should feel free to adapt activities, to add or substitute ideas of your own, or to use materials from other sources to meet the needs of any group.

The programme can be used as it stands. Individual sessions can be used on their own, or a number of them can be grouped together to meet particular needs.

It is recommended that Sessions 1 and 2 and the final session are included in any programme, although many of the other sessions can be used or left out, as necessary, to meet the needs of any group or setting. This is because the initial two sessions provide a natural framework and start a process of participants forming a community, agreeing guidelines, meeting new people and making choices that can be reflected on by group members in later sessions. The last session ends the programme by evaluating what has been learnt and setting future goals.

Each session contains the following materials:

Aims and learning outcomes

These explain the purpose of each session and what group members can expect to gain from it.

Introduction

This introduces the group leader to the thinking behind the session and discusses some issues to bear in mind.

Preparing to do the activities

Here, suggestions are provided to help you when planning group activities. There are exercises to get you thinking about the activities and to enable you to use your own experience, as well as reminders about some practical matters.

Session plan

The plan gives a summary of the session, which can be kept in front of you when running the session. It contains:

★ A reminder to review the previous session, get feedback from any homework set and to set the aims for the current session;

★ The objective for each activity;

★ The titles of the activities;

★ The approximate time each activity will take. (These times are only intended as a guide. Times will vary depending on the size of the group and the abilities of group members.);

★ A reminder to review the current session and set homework.

Activity guidelines

Detailed instructions on how to do each activity, including instructions for homework. How you present the material can be altered to suit particular groups. For example, for some groups you may wish to add additional role-play activities to aid learning.

Handouts

The handouts are designed to be photocopied and given to group members. Some are to be used during the session as part of the activity, and some are intended as notes to be given out as reminders of what has been learnt and should be given out at the end of particular activities. Others are to be worked on as homework. If you think that a handout is inappropriate you can adapt it or make up one of your own, based on the needs of the group. Some people might feel uncomfortable about completing written exercises. If this happens alternative approaches might include:

★ Having small group discussions with one person taking notes;

- ★ Having each person record their comments on a cassette recorder, which can then be kept in their portfolio;
- ★ Using a flip-chart to record group comments and then transferring these to photocopied sheets;
- ★ Providing audio recordings of handouts for group members who have difficulty with written material.

Resources

The resources required for the sessions have been kept to a minimum. However, you will need:

- ★ Folders or a file of some sort in which participants can keep a portfolio of material from the sessions, such as handouts, worksheets, self-assessment sheets and notes;
- ★ Access to a photocopier;
- ★ Paper and pens;
- ★ A flip-chart, paper and felt pens, or alternatively, a white or chalk board;
- ★ A means of pinning flip-chart sheets on walls.

Making the programme work

You will need to read through and familiarise yourself with all the information supplied before each session. Look through the suggested activities and use them to plan a session, adapting any of the materials as necessary to meet the needs of your particular group. Trying some of the activities yourself will help you decide what, if any, additional materials or adaptations you want to include. It will also help you get a feel for the activities.

Encourage discussion and participation rather than attempting to lecture the group. Remind members regularly that progress depends on putting what is learnt into practice away from the group. They will thus gain experience in the use of interaction skills they have learnt and be able to make desired changes to their lives.

PART 1

Preparing to run an interaction skills group

Introduction	9
Organising the group	11
Guidelines for success	18
Strategies to overcome common problems	22

Introduction

Individuals will have come to an interaction skills group through many different routes. Those who have a mental illness may have become socially isolated and need to learn, or re-learn, skills and regain confidence, to break social isolation and be able to establish and maintain relationships, to fulfil social roles and have their needs met.

Other group members may have some learning disabilities and need to develop their interaction skills to enable them to communicate better, to form relationships, to get a job and to be aware of how they can best interact with others.

Some groups may be comprised of young people who want to develop the skills needed to make a success of relationships in all aspects of their future lives.

Whether or not individuals are well-motivated to learn, making changes can be a major and daunting step. Facilitators need to be sensitive to group members' feelings since many of them will have poor interaction skills, few friends and may have experienced extreme social distress.

The goals of individuals in the group may include:

- Forming better relationships;
- Coping better at work;
- Sharing feelings with others;
- Controlling social anxiety.

In each case, learning to interact effectively with people around them is vital to achieving these goals.

Interacting with other people is not something constant that never changes, like cleaning teeth. It is a process that changes while it happens. As people interact, their perceptions of others and themselves alter, however subtly. Feelings, attitudes, beliefs and values may also change. When interaction goes well, people feel good about themselves. If it goes badly, confidence and self-esteem are undermined. That is why it is so important to develop good, confident interaction skills.

Interaction skills and social inclusion

Poor interaction skills can lead to a whole range of difficulties for individuals that lead to them feeling socially excluded. These difficulties may include:

- Not being able to form or sustain relationships
- Being bullied
- Always arguing with people
- Feeling ashamed
- Not understanding
- Not being able to communicate feelings or needs
- Problems getting employment
- Social isolation
- Inability to form intimate relationships
- Not managing emotions
- Not understanding another person's viewpoint
- Not trusting people
- Loneliness
- Inability to resolve conflicts
- Feeling inadequate
- Lack of self-esteem and self-confidence
- Feelings of not belonging or fitting in
- Conflict with authority
- Being thought of as a trouble-maker or as uncooperative.

Good interaction skills provide a route to feeling socially included. This includes:

- Improved self-esteem
- Better relationships
- More confidence
- Ability to resolve conflicts
- Social acceptance
- Better ability to manage emotions
- Being able to communicate feelings and needs
- Understanding other viewpoints
- Being able to form and sustain relationships
- Trusting and being trusted
- Having friends.

Cultural considerations

Do be aware of cultural differences between participants. Not all cultures place the same value on interaction behaviour. For example, direct eye contact may be considered rude in some cultures. Both group facilitators and group members will need to be aware of the different values placed on different behaviours in various cultures – particularly if any group members belong to different cultures.

Organising the group

The process outlined below can be varied to suit the demands of whatever setting you work in – school, adult learning, hospital or day centre. Select the steps that are appropriate. The stages described are generally based on recommendations provided in *Groups: Process and Practice* by Marianne Schneider Corey and Gerald Corey (5th edn, 1997, Brooks Cole Publishing Company).

Stage 1: Establishing needs

Whatever setting you work in, you should first establish evidence that an interaction group is needed. Information gathered from a needs assessment can be used to persuade colleagues and referring agencies to cooperate and support you. However, do bear in mind that an interaction group will not provide everything for everyone. Data can also be used to show accountability to authorities, group members, parents and so on. The assessment can be done by conducting a simple survey using a form, such as that provided in Appendix 1.

Stage 2: Preparing a proposal

Once the need for an interaction skills group is established, the next step is to prepare a proposal. This will detail what you are going to do and how you are going to do it. Doing this will help you to focus, to gain confidence about what you are doing and to be prepared to answer any questions you may be asked by colleagues and people referring to the group, as well as potential group members. If the group is aimed at young people, it will also be useful to present a proposal to parents or guardians if permission needs to be obtained from them, allowing them to give informed consent.

Ensure the proposal includes the following:

- The aim of the group
- A description of the group
- Who the group is for
- What needs will be met. What will individuals gain?
- What the group will do
- Topics to be covered in the group. What choice do group members have in selecting topics?
- How group members will be selected
- When and where the group will meet and for how long
- Will it be a closed or open group?
- What are the techniques to be used? (Role playing, modelling, discussion, type of exercises and so on)
- How will group members be protected both emotionally and physically?
- Are special precautions needed because of the client group?
- What confidentiality boundaries and limits are there?
- How will confidentiality boundaries be handled (Client parents, carers or relatives wanting information divulged)?
- What will be put in place for members who are not selected or drop out?
- How will success for each participant be measured?
- How will you know if your aims have been achieved?
- What follow-up will be provided?
- How will facilitator evaluation take place?
- How will evaluation data be stored? Who will have access to it?
- What problems do you expect to meet at various stages of the group and how will these be dealt with?

Stage 3: Recruiting group members

How members are recruited will depend on the setting. You may work in an environment where the potential client group can be contacted through members of your own staff group, as in day centres, colleges, adult learning or schools. It may be appropriate to have a referral system so that social workers, community psychiatric nurses, occupational therapists and other care workers can refer clients to the group. If you are targeting a particular section of the community, such as people with mental health problems or young people, this will need to be made clear on any advertising materials.

Many methods can be used to recruit members. These include:

* Posters: it is important that both staff who may refer individuals and potential clients know what is on offer, so use all available means to raise awareness. This could include staff notice boards, ward notice boards, day centre notice boards, student notice boards, libraries, coffee shops and so on. Make use of all venues used by potential clients to display posters.
* Leaflets: send these to all interested people.
* Newsletters: advertise in staff, student or client newsletters, as appropriate.
* Visits: arrange to visit staff, student or client groups that may be interested in the new group, give them information about the course and answer their questions. Personal visits of this nature can be very effective in breaking down barriers and have much greater impact then just sending out information.
* Use networks: persuade your colleagues and professional contacts to spread the word.
* Internet facilities: most authorities have their own networks. Use them to inform all interested parties.

When advertising, keep details brief, but do ensure that information sheets include the following information:

* Who the course is for: is it aimed at a particular client group, such as young people, people with a mental health problem and so on?
* What the aim of the course is: knowing this will help individuals to appreciate what they will get out of the course. Will there be any certificates awarded on completion? This will help to motivate members.
* Practical details: including where, when, what time, how long sessions will last, how many sessions and any costs.
* How to join: ensure that the address, telephone number, email address and name of the contact person for information or appointments is clear.

Stage 4: Obtaining consent

Settings such as schools, colleges and day centres are likely to have set procedures for obtaining any necessary consent from guardians or parents. Ensure that these procedures are followed.

Stage 5: Using a pre-group interview

The purpose of pre-group interviews is threefold:

- To give information to, and obtain consent from, the client;
- To ensure the individual's commitment.;
- To obtain information that will help you in the selection process.

When seeing each person, make sure he or she is given information about:

- The aims and objectives of the group;
- When and where the group meetings will take place;
- The group size;
- Group members sharing information about themselves, such as feelings, behaviour and so on. Make it clear that no one will be forced to share anything they do not want to;
- Benefits of being in the group;
- Risks involved in taking part in the group;
- Confidentiality. What happens if anyone makes disclosures about issues that can not be ignored, such as self-harming, crimes or abuse?
- Expectation about commitment to the group;
- The procedure when a person is unable to attend;
- Rules about verbal, physical or drug abuse;
- Commitment about completing homework;
- Commitment to making changes.

Find out from the client:

- What is their expectation from the group?
- Why they want to take part?
- If there are influences that could make it difficult for them at this time. (Going through a crisis, changing accommodation, lack of ability to concentrate, acute anxiety or depression).

Throughout the process, keep summarising and asking questions to ensure that the information you are giving is being understood.

When the interview has been completed you should know if the person:

- Has understood the aims and objectives;
- Will be able to understand the level of content to be covered in the group;
- Wants to be a member of the group;
- Has some positive abilities from which other group members can learn;
- Is motivated;
- Is going along with the process, rather than making a commitment;

- ★ Understands the need to be committed to making changes, and the feelings of discomfort that will be encountered at times when working through their difficulties;
- ★ Understands influences that might hinder progress;
- ★ Has any special needs (literacy ability, learning disability, physical disability and so on).

The above information should help you to select the clients who will benefit most from the sessions. It is also essential knowledge to have when planning the content of the course to enable you to decide:

- ★ The level at which to pitch the course;
- ★ Which teaching aids will be useful;
- ★ Which teaching methods will work best;
- ★ What language level to use;
- ★ What examples will be required, and how many;
- ★ Which modelling exercises to prepare;
- ★ What support is needed for individuals.

Stage 6: Selecting group members

It is important that the process allows you to select group members from whom others in the group can learn appropriate behaviour. If everyone displays the same negative behaviour there will be no positive models from whom to learn and learning may be impeded. For example, if everyone has the same difficulty with being assertive, there will be no one from whom to learn how to overcome that particular difficulty.

It is important to avoid selecting group members who:

- ★ Have extreme differences in abilities and learning experiences (such as mixing someone with learning disabilities, a university student or someone with literacy problems and someone from an ethnic minority);
- ★ Are abusive verbally or physically;
- ★ Are undergoing a crisis (unless the group is in response to that crisis).

Do let prospective clients know whether or not they have been chosen. Some may interpret not being selected as a rejection. Counteract this by:

- ★ Making it clear in advertising and initial discussions that not everyone may be included in the group;
- ★ Planning a group at a later date to meet the needs of those who cannot be included this time;

- Explaining the reasons why potential members will not be selected (such as undergoing a crisis);
- Being prepared to refer individuals to more appropriate services such as individual counselling.

Stage 7: Using an initial evaluation

An initial evaluation enables the group facilitator to find out if individuals or the group as a whole have benefited from the group session. Self-assessment forms are supplied at group sessions and will give some general information. These measures are intended to provide both group facilitators and group members with some indication of what progress has been made.

Stage 8: Managing the sessions

The length of group sessions, and their number, can be adjusted to fit individuals' schedules. It is recommended that at least eight sessions are taken – this will allow the dynamics of group processes to take place. Groups go through several stages.

Forming

At this stage people are very unsure of other group members. They need to get to know each other and learn to feel at ease and work together. There may be feelings of anxiety, and individuals may be waiting for others to begin the work.

Storming

Tensions and conflict can build up. There may be personality clashes, disputes about the aims of the group and challenges to the group leader. Individuals may be feeling threatened or uncomfortable. Their thoughts may be 'This isn't working', 'I'm not going to do this' or 'This is too much'. This nearly always happens in some way and can be a minor turbulence, which is easily overcome, or something of a storm. Whichever scenario it is, use the event to develop a process of dealing openly with conflict when it arises. This can serve to strengthen the acceptance of conflict and working through differences.

Norming

This is the process of the group establishing 'norms', of group cohesion and learning to work cooperatively together and establishing methods to solve problems. Individuals will have an incentive to stay in the group and will have a sense of belonging. Examples of norms are group members:

- Giving feedback to each other;
- Expecting everyone to attend regularly;
- Sharing feelings;
- Bringing individual problems to the group;
- Supporting each other;
- Providing challenges for other group members to look at and work through.

Performing

Group members have settled in at this stage and will be getting on with the task. Trust will have been built. Individuals feel safe taking risks and are able to share feelings and accept each other. A sense of cohesion exists and members feel they are getting on with the tasks of the group and are working towards their aims.

Stage 9: Using an end-of-course evaluation

Do this before the group sessions finish, using the same evaluation as used at the beginning of the sessions. This will give a measure of how individuals perceive improvement in their interaction behaviour.

Stage 10: Follow up and final evaluation

Conducting a follow-up evaluation will enable group leaders to see the effectiveness of continued learning after the group has concluded. Arrange for group members to meet again in six to 12 weeks' time, or arrange to send evaluation forms to them. Doing this enables clients to share their accomplishments, to discuss how they have continued working on issues covered in the group sessions, to encourage each other and to renew their commitment to achieving changes in their interaction behaviour.

Data gathered will also provide information on the effectiveness of the group, for reporting to authorities and making improvements in any future groups. A brief written report outlining the results and describing the experience will be adequate for most settings. Do remember that data from these evaluations should remain confidential and information shared with others for accountability purposes should not contain identifiable information.

Guidelines for success

Thinking about the group size

The desirable number of people in a group will be dictated by a number of influences. If using one group facilitator, about eight to 10 group members allows each person an opportunity to participate actively and enables them to express their ideas and feelings. More than this number can make it difficult for a person who is shy, lacks assertiveness or is anxious to participate. On the other hand, fewer than six people will not allow enough diversity of interaction and can place too much pressure on individuals to contribute. Also, more than 10 group members make it difficult for a single group facilitator to keep track of what is happening and provides less time for each person to contribute.

Using two group facilitators has advantages. They can share knowledge and give each other feedback on what is happening in the group. Individual support can be given more easily to any group members who need it. For groups that have more than 10 members, a co-worker is essential.

In some settings, such as mental health, it may be expedient to allow for some absenteeism and those who may drop out by recruiting a few extra members to the group.

Finding a suitable venue

Because of the confidential nature of groupwork, a venue should be chosen where other people will not be able to overhear what is said and the group will not be disturbed. Attention to the following details will help ensure the success of the group.

- ★ Is the room large enough to seat everyone in comfort? It is best if group members can sit in a circle, including the leader, so that all participants can see and hear each other clearly.
- ★ Is there enough space to be able to use flip-charts or a chalk-board, and for the group to break up into smaller units to do exercises?
- ★ Is the room suitable for people with disabilities or special needs? Is there a loop system for anyone with a hearing impairment?

- ★ Will anyone with disabilities be able to access toilets without embarrassment or disturbing other members of the group?
- ★ Is the room reasonably quiet?
- ★ Are there power points to enable use of audio-visual aids if you want to use them?
- ★ Can drinks be made in the room, if required, during the break?

Deciding the number and the format of sessions

The number of group sessions may be dictated by issues such as time available and the ability of individuals in the group. For this reason, sessions are presented in a flexible manner. For example, if the needs of individuals can be met by eight sessions, then hold eight sessions. Time constraints, or having to fit into a curriculum, may also mean that the number of sessions must be limited. The programme and format can be adjusted to suit particular circumstances. Alternatively, the complete programme can be used. However, it is sensible that the groups meet on a weekly basis at a time convenient to their members.

Considering ethical issues

It is not within the scope of this book to discuss the full complexities of ethical issues in groupwork. However, it is important to point out that group facilitators have a responsibility to adhere to ethical practice regarding the issues of confidentiality, participants' rights and any psychological or physical risks taken. Group facilitators should bear in mind the guidelines of any professional organisations to which they belong.

The sessions in this book are designed to explore feelings about how individuals see themselves, how they view their interaction skills and how they fit into their personal, social and work communities. It is possible that some activities may inadvertently trigger disclosures or emotions that are outside the scope of the group – especially in individuals who may have been abused or have behavioural or emotional disorders. Tactfully suggest that these issues may be better addressed outside the group and, if necessary, with appropriate specialists.

Modelling

Modelling is a process of observational learning. Group members learn new interaction skills by watching someone else (group facilitators) demonstrate them. The group leader can draw the attention of participants to the process and discuss each step demonstrated. Group members can then practise their skills in role play.

Modelling is very effective with individuals who find verbal feedback difficult, who have literacy problems, some learning disabilities and with people with mental illness. Use lots of modelling with these group members and provide many opportunities to practise skills. This enables the process to become automatic.

Giving feedback

Feedback is the response given, verbally – directly, or non-verbally indirectly – by other members of the group during and after a role play or exercise. By listening to what is being said and by noting how other members behave during and after an interaction, group members learn something about how the interaction has been perceived by others. An example would be if a person made a statement, thinking that he was being kind and supportive, but the statement was seen by other group members as patronising. This may be perceived in both non-verbal in feedback – in the body language of how the other people reacted – and verbal feedback, by what they say.

If group members are encouraged to share their thoughts and feelings about interactions it will help them to build trust in each other and the group.

All this information (feedback) is useful to each person in becoming aware of what effect their interactions have, and it can be used to enable them to guide future interactions. It also makes them aware that this information is available to them in their day-to-day interactions and relationships, and that they can make use of it to improve those relationships.

Discourage group members from making destructive statements that are disguised as feedback. If members do this, ask them to follow the same process discussed under 'Negative and destructive remarks' in the next chapter (p23).

Evaluating as you go

It is important that there is an opportunity for group members and facilitators to reflect on how the course is going so that changes to the content and format can be made if necessary.

Plan in time for group members to air their views about the course, the activities, the methods being used and how the group is working.

This can be done in an informal way at set stages of the course, perhaps at the end of a session. Alternatively, you can use a more formal approach, using a questionnaire or setting an activity, or perhaps by splitting the group members into small groups or pairs for discussion and then having them give feedback to the whole group.

These evaluations can be used as examples of people participating and being involved in a community and contributing in a positive way to its success.

Using self-disclosure

Group leaders are encouraged to reflect on their own interaction experiences when preparing the activities, as a means of thinking through how best to approach an activity and to appreciate how group members may be feeling. This is not a licence to use lots of personal self-disclosures in a group. Revealing something about how you are thinking or feeling to the group can be helpful, but it needs to be approached with caution. Use self-disclosure:

- To model making disclosures. Do this by reflecting on how the group is going: 'I don't think this activity is going well! Does anyone agree?'; 'I'm finding this hard going. How do you feel about it?'; and 'I learned a lot from that. How did you find it?'.
- If an event from your own experience can be used to get a discussion going, it should be relevant to the activity and could, for example, demonstrate how you learnt something from a bad interaction experience.

If you use self-disclosure, ensure it is to benefit the group members and not to make yourself the focus of attention. Do not share personal or confidential information about other people.

Avoiding failure

Having an initial interview, paying attention to detail, involving group members in setting the guidelines and planning for the group, all help to ensure success. Ongoing evaluations and ensuring that everyone has an action plan for the conclusion of the group, to continue their progress as outlined, will combine to ensure that:

- The course learning materials are appropriate;
- Motivation is helped by making clear what will be expected from group members and what each person wants to achieve on the course;
- Expectations are realistic;
- Participants are clear that improvement in their interaction skills is dependent on their efforts;
- The course is set at an appropriate level;
- The group can be used as a model for participants wanting to build better support networks and improve their interactions in community groups within their family groups, socially or at work.

Strategies to overcome common problems

All groups have problems at some time. Facilitators may not always be able to prevent them, but they will need to deal with them when they occur. Here are some common issues that may be encountered.

Straying from the activity topic

If this happens, bring the focus back to the topic. Explain that constant off-topic discussion can disrupt or make it difficult to follow the train of thought the group needs to follow. It may also leave insufficient time to complete the material to be covered in the session.

Group members want the group facilitator to provide all the answers

Enable the group to adapt a problem-solving participation by redirecting comments or questions back to the group. This can be achieved by saying things like: 'What do other group members feel about this?', or 'One or two of you have had similar experiences. How did you deal with it?'. This promotes group involvement.

Alternatively, write the question or statement on a flip-chart and use brainstorming techniques to promote participation and a problem-solving attitude. This enables all group members to participate in the process of problem solving.

Negative and destructive remarks

Explain that negative and destructive remarks can be hurtful, may hinder progress, interfere with communication and are generally unhelpful. Ask individuals to put criticism in a way that is constructive and is not delivered in a 'put-down' manner. Give examples of put-downs, for example: 'What an idiot!', or 'How stupid are you!'. The manner or tone in which criticism is made can make it a put-down. In order for criticism to be constructive it should:

- Start with something positive;
- State the problem;
- Provide a possible solution.

Examples might be: 'I understand what you want me to do, but there will not be enough time on Tuesday. I could do it on Friday'; 'The idea is good but I don't think you should do it on your own. Could we do it together?'.

It can be helpful to have a brief discussion about how individuals feel after being 'put down'. How does it make people feel about each other?

Anxiety and lack of group cohesion

If individuals can see that other group members have difficulties and concerns similar to their own it will help to reduce anxiety and will increase group cohesion. Promote this by helping everyone to share concerns. Use questions like: 'Does anybody else feel like that?', 'How many of you have had a similar experience?', or 'Did any of you do something different when you experienced the same thing?'.

Doing this will help to dispel apprehension within the group and will enable members to identify and bond with each other. Other methods that can help include:

- Ensuring that all group members are as involved as possible. Encourage anyone who is not contributing by asking for their opinion on something being discussed and how they feel while doing something. Be careful not to pressure anyone. Do bear in mind that they might just be confused, may not understand or be inclined to learn though listening and watching.
- Asking open questions and checking personal experience when giving information. This also helps to avoid continuous lecturing, which often makes it difficult for people to feel involved.
- Encouraging group members to comment and congratulate each other when exercises or tasks have been completed.

Group members have difficulty understanding information being given

Assist group members' understanding by using a variety of presentation methods. Flip-charts or chalk-boards are good for brainstorming, showing diagrams or flowcharts. Showing handouts on an overhead projector can work well. Drawing simple diagrams or cartoons to illustrate key issues can make material more memorable.

Visual aids can take time to prepare, but are well worth the effort. One drawing can often put across a concept that remains confusing after several attempts at verbal explanation.

Use modelling and role-play. Explain verbally, then demonstrate interaction behaviour and ask group members to role-play it. Visual aids, modelling and role-plays are particularly important when any group members have some learning disabilities, literacy problems, or when working with adolescents. Concepts and terminology should also be kept simple.

Summarise. Stop at regular intervals and summarise what has been learnt, or ask group members to summarise their learning in their own words.

Clarify. If group members do not understand a concept, then explain it in a way that is more comprehensible to them. Make sure that the words and terms used are ones with which they are familiar.

Individuals feel uncomfortable

Areas that are uncomfortable for some participants may be touched on. This sometimes results in disclosures being made. Take care not to force anyone further than they want to go. If a person shows signs of agitation or discomfort with particular issues or topics, accept their decision on how far they want to participate or what they want to disclose. They can listen to what other people have to say without contributing themselves.

Interacting with other people involves feelings and emotions – expressing these opens all sorts of possibilities. But it remains the participants' choice whether or not to express them. Accept what individuals feel they can give.

Dealing with emotion

An activity or discussion can sometimes provoke an emotional response in an individual. This may be caused by reflecting on a past experience that triggers painful memories, resulting in tears or in the person wanting to leave the room. Different situations will require different responses. Here are a few suggestions.

- Reassure the person that it is OK to show emotion in the group.
- It may be helpful to create a coffee break to deal with the situation or to break tension.
- If the group has two co-workers, one worker can take the person out of the group if necessary, for a chat, a coffee or a short walk.
- If the person has a particular friend in the group, that friend might like to help with reassurance or take the person out for a coffee or a short walk.
- Acknowledge with the group what has happened. Ask the other group members how they are feeling – they may be concerned about the person. Discuss strategies for the group to support anyone who becomes upset in the future. Do this by asking members how they like to be treated when they feel upset. Some will like a few minutes on their own to compose themselves, others will like to be comforted by someone. There will be many different strategies to consider.
- Have a follow-up chat with the person after the group. There may be an issue that requires following through by a specialist professional such as a counsellor.

Interacting with other people involves expressing feelings of anger, frustration and rejection. Some participants may disclose extremely sensitive issues, such as abuse, self-harm, suicide or domestic violence. An interaction group is not a suitable forum to handle these issues and individuals will need to be referred to appropriate professionals to have suitable support provided.

Dealing with behavioural problems

A group can sometimes be disrupted by a particular group member. They may ask a question that the group facilitator is unable to answer. The facilitator should not be afraid to say that they do not know. Someone else in the group may be able to provide the answer, or the group members can use their problem-solving skills. It may mean the group leader does some research and provides the answer in the next session.

Difficult behaviour is often a defence. It may be because a person is feeling anxious or threatened. It may also be a reaction to an event or situation that has nothing to do with the group. Perhaps an individual is bored or has not been able to build enough trust to feel able to participate.

One group member may continually try to dominate discussions. A ground rule that each person is given a limited time to state their view can ensure that everyone has an opportunity to comment. Alternatively, the group leader can intervene, thank the dominant person for expressing their view and ask someone else to comment. Splitting a large group up into small sub-groups or to work in pairs will help prevent a particular person from dominating.

If the behaviour persists, it may be necessary to challenge the person about it. This is usually best done outside the group. De-personalise the issue, criticise the behaviour not the person. Say something like: 'You have made a lot of interesting comments, but you are not giving other group members opportunity to express their view. Could you keep your comments brief or allow some of the others to comment before you make your contribution?'

Sometime a group may be silent or unresponsive. The leader should attempt to understand what the group is communicating when this happens. It may be being defensive. Barriers may not have been sufficiently broken down. Perhaps it is lack of awareness on the part of the group facilitator that has triggered group members to feel as they do. Questions leaders should ask themselves include:

- ☆ Do people feel safe?
- ☆ Have I made promises that can't be kept?
- ☆ Has anything happened outside the group?
- ☆ Have I been listening to what people are saying?

One way to get the group moving is for group leaders to disclose something about how they are feeling. For example, 'I feel that the session is not going very well. I found the last exercise difficult and feel that some issues were left unanswered for some of you. Can you help me with this so we can work out how to put it right?'. The problem may still exist, but if people are encouraged to bring the problem out into the open it can be worked on.

Sometimes group members will want to criticise someone who is absent. Avoid this by pointing out that it is unfair to talk about group members when they are not present to put their point of view or defend their position.

There may be a direct and aggressive challenge to the group leader's ability: 'What are your qualifications for doing this?', or 'Have you run any groups like this before?' Direct attacks like this can be disconcerting. It is best to avoid being defensive and to give an informative reply in an honest and straightforward way, giving any experience as appropriate. It is likely that some group members are feeling threatened or worried that the leader will have difficulty handling the group or feelings that may be exposed. A question such as: 'What worries you about this?' can bring out what is behind the aggression and alleviate any fears about how the leader will handle difficult situations.

Overcoming literacy difficulties

Some group members may have different degrees of literacy difficulties. The group leader needs to be aware and deal with any problems. Depending on the degree of the literacy problem, individuals are likely to struggle with any written instruction and to use tactics to cover their embarrassment. These may include:

- Covering work sheets;
- Copying from other group members;
- Failing to complete written work;
- Becoming aggressive or displaying other behavioural tactics to avoid embarrassment;
- Reluctance to do written work. They may give reasons each week, such as 'I have left my spectacles at home'.

These individuals will need step-by-step instructions, given clearly with many pauses, to check their understanding of what is being explained and lots of examples should be given to them. It will be helpful for them to work with a partner or a group helper. Add additional modelling examples to the programme where possible. A tape recording can be used to provide the person with notes and the main learning points of the session. If written answers are required, the person can record their answers.

The group leader will also need to refer the person to services that will help them to improve their literacy skills.

Discomfort with role play

The exercises in some of the sessions include role play. Most people will display some anxiety about taking part in role play, especially if they are going to be observed. To allay fears, it is helpful to explain the purpose of role play and to give members an opportunity to share their anxieties. For the purposes of this course, it is not acting, but a process that gives individuals the chance to work through situations and try new ways of dealing with interaction problems within a safe environment. This allows them to make mistakes and learn from them. During the process, group members will experience some of the same feelings and inhibitions they would have if it was a real-life situation. Doing role play in this way enables feedback to be given and participants to discuss how they can manage interactions more effectively.

When discussion gets stuck

Sometimes in groups no one has anything to say. Everyone feels uneasy and there is an anxious atmosphere. When this occurs something has usually happened to make people feel anxious. Individuals may be worrying and find it difficult to speak out. This can happen if an emotional or difficult subject has been approached and not enough trust has been developed in the group for members to be able to handle it.

If this occurs, or if the group gets 'stuck' for any other reason, try:

- ☆ Talking about what you think is wrong. Talking about a problem often helps people to feel easier. Approach the subject by saying something like: 'I think some of you are feeling a bit uncomfortable because …'
- ☆ Asking the group members what they think is wrong.
- ☆ Dividing the group into small groups of two or three people and having them discuss what they think is wrong and then asking them to feedback to the whole group.
- ☆ Going back to safe topics on a less personal level until more trust has been gained and people feel safer, if you think the group members are feeling threatened.

Poor attendance

If someone does not attend, they will need to be contacted. If the group is not appropriate for the person at this time, perhaps due to outside circumstances, care needs to be taken to ensure that they do not feel that they have failed and that the group leader does not hold this against them. If someone is being put off by something to do with the group, this needs to be addressed. They may need additional support, the presentation methods may not match their learning style, they may have felt excluded or they may have found it overwhelming. Whatever the reason, it should be investigated and addressed. To fail to contact the person may be interpreted as if they are not worth bothering with and produce a negative outcome.

PART 2

Positive interaction skills sessions

1	Introducing positive interaction skills	33
2	Exploring social perception	45
3	Recognising influences on interaction	59
4	Developing support networks	73
5	Understanding body language	85
6	Making conversation	95
7	Learning to listen	107
8	Starting, sustaining and ending friendships	119
9	Establishing and keeping close relationships	129
10	Appreciating other points of view	141
11	Creating trust and learning to self-disclose	153
12	Resolving conflict in relationships	165
13	Being assertive and handling criticism	177
14	Overcoming shyness and loneliness	193
15	Building confidence and self-esteem	209
16	Managing emotions	221
17	Improving self-management skills	233
18	Ending the group	247

1. Introducing positive interaction skills

Aim

To welcome group members, help them feel at ease, introduce them to each other and the course, and enable them to begin working together as a group.

Learning Objectives

By the end of the session group members will:

☆ Have started to get to know each other;

☆ Have begun to bond and work together as a group;

☆ Be aware of the aims of the course and its content;

☆ Have shared what they want from the course;

☆ Understand the negotiation process to have their needs met;

☆ Have contributed to ground rules for the group;

☆ Have become more aware of the need to interact with other people.

Introduction

It is of paramount importance that the first session goes well. You need to be clear about – and keep a focus on – your aims. The session will set the tone and attitudes for the rest of the course. You should ensure that group members:

☆ Are made welcome;
☆ Feel comfortable and at ease;
☆ Are introduced to each other;
☆ Understand why they are there and the content of the course;
☆ Have their awareness raised about the need for good interaction skills;
☆ Are enabled to bond and begin working together.

Preparing to do the activities

Welcoming group members

It is helpful to think of a time when you joined a new group, class, club or society. What were your thoughts, feelings and anxieties? Were you worried about:

- What to do or say?
- What impression you might make?
- Looking or sounding foolish or silly?
- How you would cope?
- What the whole thing was about?
- Meeting new people?

Some group members may have previously had bad experiences of groups, lack confidence or self-esteem, be shy or have difficulty mixing with other people. Even if you feel confident and have good interaction skills, going into situations similar to that of a new group can make you feel nervous and uncertain. How much more acute will be the feelings of individuals who are lacking in skills and confidence – many of them may have other contributing factors to deal with, such as mental illness.

Your task is to enable group members to talk about their feelings, to reassure them and to make sure that they feel comfortable and safe.

The first step in this process is to provide a friendly greeting, to ensure that the environment is comfortable and to make all the practical arrangements clear. Be sure to include in this the structure of the sessions: that there will be open discussion and some role play. A clear structure will provide security for group members. Knowing the structure and how the group will work helps them to understand both what you expect from them and their personal responsibility within group boundaries.

Ice-breaker exercise

The next step is helping people get to know each other. Make the ice-breaker activity light-hearted and fun. Once initial introductions have been achieved and people are feeling more comfortable, you can move on to the next activity.

Ground rules

Sharing fears and worries as part of forming the ground rules is very important. It enables individuals to become aware that there are others in the same situation as themselves, who have similar fears. You can aid the process by expressing some of your own worries and acknowledging that doing this can be difficult. Do listen carefully at this point to what people say. Show you have listened by acknowledging and validating their anxiety.

Explain that this is a course in which everyone is encouraged to take part and to contribute and learn from their own experience and that of other group members. The reason for this is that groups:

- Are an ideal setting for promoting interpersonal skills;
- Provide a natural context for interaction to take place;
- Provide opportunity for people to receive and give support;
- Enable individuals to become aware that other people have interaction difficulties.

As the course progresses, group members will have an opportunity to become aware of themselves helping other group members with their interaction difficulties. People who have poor interaction skills may not have had the opportunity to see themselves in this way before. This giving and receiving of support can help individuals to develop a better self-image. It enables people to feel good about themselves. The process also helps to build trust between group members.

Why are you here?

When people start the course they will have many questions in their minds, not least:

- What is the course about?
- What am I going to be asked to do?
- How will the course help me?

The 'Why are you here?' activity gives an opportunity for group members to discuss why they are attending the group to interact and to begin building relationships by making disclosures about themselves. Both the ice-breaker activity and this one will have started them on that process.

What is being offered?

The interaction problems highlighted in the 'Why are you here?' activity can easily be linked to the sessions outlined in Handout 1, and the negotiation process can start to ensure that the issues group members feel are most relevant to them are included. You can point out that they have already started to practise many of the skills that will be covered during the course.

Why positive interaction skills?

This is an awareness exercise that is likely to:

- Raise discomfort levels and dissatisfaction levels with areas that individuals find difficult;
- Enable individuals to see the benefits of working on their skills and what these will mean to them.

Acknowledge the discomfort people may feel during discussions about the interaction areas they have difficulty with. This, combined with the benefits to be achieved by completing the course, will help to provide motivation for individuals to continue, to work hard and to stay with the discomfort they will feel at times during the course. If anyone begins to lose motivation during the course, it is worthwhile going over areas that they feel are difficult, bringing out the discomfort and dissatisfaction they feel, looking at the benefits that they can achieve and using this to keep them motivated.

Homework

Explain to the group that the homework is devised to enable them to put the skills they will be learning into practice. If learning is to be any use, it must be put into practice in their daily lives. This will feel uncomfortable and awkward at times – this is normal and to be expected – but this feeling will dissipate with practice and as their confidence grows.

1. Introducing interaction skills

Objectives	Activity	Time (in mins)
To make everyone feel welcome, to go through practical arrangements and to introduce the aims of the group	**Welcome and practical arrangements**	15
To help group members get to know each other and put them at ease	**Ice-breaker exercise**	15
To agree some ground rules that will help group members to feel comfortable	**Ground rules**	15
BREAK		10
To give group members an opportunity to discuss their reasons for attending the course and state what they want from it	**Why are you here?**	25
To make group members aware of the course content and what choices are available to them	**What is being offered?**	10
To make group members more aware of the need for good interaction skills	**Why positive interaction skills?**	25
To check that outcomes have been achieved and explain the homework assignments	**Review the session and set homework assignment**	5

1. Activity guidelines

Welcome and practical arrangements

When everyone has arrived and settled down, start with a few words of welcome. The group members should feel that you know something about them and why they are attending the course. This can be achieved by mentioning the aim of the course. Here is an example:

> **Aim:** to enable individuals to develop and sustain relationships with other people in their personal, social and work life.
>
> **By:** developing their interaction skills, confidence and self-esteem.
>
> **Through:** sharing information, learning from personal experience, discussion and exercises.

Session 1: Introducing positive interaction skills — 37

It is helpful to write the chosen aim on a flip-chart sheet and put it up on a wall so that it can remain on view throughout the session.

Next, run through the practical arrangements. These should include:

- Fire procedure;
- Where the toilets are;
- General comfort in the room – too hot or cold;
- Refreshments (if any);
- Seating arrangements;
- Times of the sessions – check that the time of the day is convenient;
- How long each session is and if there are any breaks;
- The structure of the sessions and homework;
- Explaining the use of discussion, role play, brainstorming and feedback in learning from experience.

This is also a good opportunity to ask group members to bring up any practical problems they may have. You can ask them to see you after the group if there is anything they do not feel able to discuss in the group. Give out any folders for people to keep notes in.

Finish the welcoming activity by telling them the aim of this first session and what the learning outcome will be. This will lead into the second activity.

Ice-breaker exercises

If the group members do not know each other or the group is fairly large, choose one of the following exercises that will help them to remember each other's names. If they do know each other, pick an ice-breaker activity that will help to establish a friendly atmosphere, enables people get to know each other better, puts them at their ease and breaks down any barriers. You may choose to use an exercise you know that has worked well for you in the past instead of one of the following:

Ice-breaker 1

Ask group members to split into pairs. They then spend about two minutes finding out three things about their partner. Reassemble everyone again and ask group members, in turn, to introduce their partner to the group, stating the person's name and the three things they have learnt about them. You can make it easier by writing the three things to be found on the flip-chart. An example would be:

- Where they were born;
- A hobby or game they enjoy;
- Who they most admire.

Ice-breaker 2

Ask group members, in turn, to name an animal that represents how they are feeling. Encourage each person to expand on their statement as they make it. What is it about the animal that expresses the feeling? Some may merely want to state the name of the animal. Do not force anyone to expand on the feeling if they are reluctant to do so. But usually other people will identify with the feeling and help them. Objects or flowers can be used instead of animals.

Ice-breaker 3

Have everyone sitting in a circle. Each player, in turn, states their name. Now one person calls out someone else's name and throws a soft ball or cushion to them. That person catches the item, calls out another name and throws the item to them. The game continues in this way until everyone's name has been repeated a few times. If anyone is in doubt about someone's name, stop, ask the person their name and then throw the ball to them. A simple but fun game that loosens inhibitions and enables people to become familiar with each other's names.

Ground rules

Ground rules are important in creating an atmosphere of confidence and trust within the group – especially when personal information is to be shared. Rules must be agreed by the whole group. As the group progresses they may want to add one or two extra items to deal with issues that occur. Ground rules are usually built around worries that people might have about the group. These issues may include:

- Confidentiality – should everything said within the group be kept confidential to the group?
- Everyone having the right to express their opinion and to have it respected – even though the opinion may not be shared by other group members.
- Not being pressured to say or do anything they feel uncomfortable about.
- Supporting each other.
- Not interrupting each other.
- An agreement that people will make the effort to turn up on time.

It can be helpful to have group members call out any worries that they may have. These worries can be discussed and turned into ground rules for the group. They should be turned into statements and written on a flip-chart. For example:

> - We will keep everything said confidential to the group;
> - We will respect each other's opinions;
> - We will not pressure anyone to say or do anything they feel uncomfortable with;
> - We will all make an effort to get here on time;
> - We will review the ground rules every six weeks.

Once written on a flip-chart sheet, the rules can be displayed at each session as a reminder, or, alternatively, typed on a sheet and handed out to everyone. It is a good idea to review the ground rules at intervals, since this reminds people about what they have agreed and also provides an opportunity to add new rules to deal with any additional worries that may have come to light.

Why are you here?

If you are working with a large group, split the members into smaller subgroups of three or four people. If the group is small, divide everyone into pairs. If using pairs, ensure that people are not paired with the same people as in any previous exercise.

Ask people in the subgroups to spend two or three minutes talking about their reasons for attending the group and what they want from it. Discussion may bring out statements such as: 'I find it really difficult to get to know new people. I never know what to talk about and always feel uncomfortable', or 'I make friends easily enough but I can't hold on to them. I fall out with them and they don't want anything to do with me'.

Once the allocated time is up, bring the group back together again and ask each person to state why they are attending the group. Summarise the statements on a flip-chart. Examples may be:

> - I want to overcome my shyness;
> - I want to be able to make friends;
> - I want to be able to keep my friends;
> - I want to be able to resolve conflicts I get into.

When this has been completed, point out all the needs that are similar and can be worked on in the group. Keep the flip-chart sheet so that the group can review their goals in the final session.

What is being offered?

This activity clarifies the areas that can be covered on the course. Give out and talk through Handout 1. Explain that Sessions 1, 2 and the final session will definitely be included, but that the others are open to negotiation, depending on the number of weeks available to run the course. Ask group members to tick the sessions they particularly want and to put a cross in the box of any they do not want.

You may have to stress the importance of particular sessions and explain that if you are restricted to a small number of sessions, some group members may not be able to have all the options they choose. Tell them that you will look at their choices before the next session and produce a set programme for the rest of the course. Say that you will do your best to accommodate everyone's needs based on the previous activity and this one. End the activity by collecting the forms.

Why positive interaction skills?

Ask the group to brainstorm what they understand by the term 'positive interaction skills' and to write the statements on a flip-chart. Now break the group up into three subgroups.

> Ask Group 1 to discuss:
>   * How poor interaction skills can affect personal and home relationships.
>   * How good interaction skills can affect personal and home relationships.
>
> Ask Group 2 to discuss:
>   * How poor interaction skills can affect their social life.
>   * How good interaction skills can affect their social life.
>
> Ask Group 3 to discuss:
>   * How poor interaction skills can affect them at work.
>   * How good interaction skills can affect them at work.

Give each group a large sheet of paper and a magic marker and have them write their main points on the sheet. When completed, bring everyone back together again and have a member from each subgroup feedback their findings to the whole group.

Reviewing the session and setting homework

Go though the learning outcomes stating what has been achieved:

- People have started to get to know each other;
- Ground rules have been agreed;
- The aims of the course have been made clear;
- People have shared what they want from the course;
- The course contents have been discussed;
- Awareness has been raised of the benefits from, and need for, good interaction skills.

In discussions, have any particular problems emerged that need to be solved before the next session? State them and how you will solve them. Is there anything that you need to follow up on? State anything and what your actions will be.

For homework, give out Handout 2 and explain that you would like everyone to fill in the form. It is important that people are honest with themselves when doing the rating. They will be asked to fill in a similar form again at the end of the course. This will enable them to see how much their skills have improved and will provide an indication of how successful the course has been.

Handout 1 What is on offer?

Sessions

Introducing positive interaction skills

Exploring social perception

Optional sessions

Choose which sessions will meet your need for learning by ticking the appropriate boxes.

- Recognising influences on interaction ☐
- Developing support networks ☐
- Understanding body language ☐
- Making conversation ☐
- Learning to listen ☐
- Starting, sustaining and ending friendships ☐
- Establishing and keeping close relationships ☐
- Appreciating other points of view ☐
- Creating trust and learning to self-disclose ☐
- Resolving conflict in relationships ☐
- Being assertive and handling criticism ☐
- Overcoming shyness and loneliness ☐
- Building confidence and self-esteem ☐
- Managing emotions ☐
- Improving self-management skills ☐

Final session

Ending the group

Handout 2 Skills evaluation

Rate your abilities in the following areas:	Poor				Good
Recognising influences on how people interact	1	2	3	4	5
Developing supportive social networks	1	2	3	4	5
Understanding body language	1	2	3	4	5
Making conversation	1	2	3	4	5
Listening to others	1	2	3	4	5
Starting, sustaining and ending relationships	1	2	3	4	5
Establishing and keeping close relationships	1	2	3	4	5
Appreciating other points of view	1	2	3	4	5
Creating trust and learning to self-disclose	1	2	3	4	5
Resolving conflict in relationships	1	2	3	4	5
Being assertive and handling criticism	1	2	3	4	5
Overcoming shyness and loneliness	1	2	3	4	5
Building confidence and self-esteem	1	2	3	4	5
Managing emotions	1	2	3	4	5
Self-management	1	2	3	4	5

My strengths are:

Areas I need to improve are:

2 Exploring social perception

Aim

To enable group members to become more aware that how they interact with other people and how they feel about themselves relates to the communities (clubs, societies, family groups) in which they participate and live.

Learning Objectives

By the end of the session group members will understand:

- What communities are about;
- Why they live in communities;
- How they feel about themselves relates to how they interact in communities;
- How communities work;
- What life would be like without communities;
- What communities they belong to;
- Their responsibility to decide what communities they want to belong to.

Introduction

Exploring social perception makes group members aware of how they interact with other people and how they feel about themselves relates to the communities in which they live. It helps them to:

- Understand the importance of developing good interaction skills;
- Become motivated to improve their skills;
- Appreciate the important effect communities have on the way they feel about themselves;
- Become aware how important belonging to communities is to their development.

Going through this process is particularly important for people who live isolated lives, who have become withdrawn from mixing in communities or who do not have the opportunity to take part in community life.

When preparing to lead the group, consider how nervous you might feel if you had to share some of the required answers with a group. What would help you as a group member to do this? What can you do as group facilitator to ensure that group members will feel safe sharing their thoughts?

Preparing to do the activities

Reviewing the session and obtaining feedback from homework

Reviewing the main points of the previous session reminds people of what they have learnt. Asking them how they managed their homework assignment creates the expectation that homework assignments will be completed, shows interest and enables group members to support each other. It is important that this happens at the beginning of each session.

What are communities?

This exercise, as outlined in the Activity Guidelines, will help learners become aware of, and understand, the many types of community everyone experiences – from the family unit, to social and more formal groups.

Why live in communities?

If you have thought through the many communities you belong to and the benefits you derive from them, it will help you to draw out benefits from the group members. Also, ask yourself how important these communities are to you and in what way they provide support.

Self-esteem and communities

Are there ways in which the communities you belong to boost your self-esteem? How would you be affected if you did not belong to those communities? Raising group members' awareness of these issues will help to place them in a better position to make informed judgements about the value of belonging to communities, motivating them to learn the skills needed to interact with others and to have satisfactory relationships.

How communities work

When preparing for this activity, bear in mind communities you have joined, including the current group. Ask yourself the following questions:

- ★ Are there basic rules or guidelines to be kept?
- ★ How have these guidelines been decided?

- ☆ What happens when someone displays unwanted behaviour?
- ☆ Do people need to coopcrate with each other?
- ☆ What interaction skills are required by individuals in the community to communicate how they feel and what they want?
- ☆ Are skills like assertiveness, listening, making conversation, appreciating other viewpoints, resolving conflict and so on required?
- ☆ Are these issues also true of societies and nations?

Communities I belong to

This activity is intended to enable learners to explore their own personal communities and how these limit or expand their opportunities. It will place them in a more informed position to decide what communities they would like to belong to and to explore any hindrances related to their ability to interact successfully with others.

Completing the exercise for your own situation will provide you with a good idea of how group members will feel doing the exercise and what difficulties they might encounter.

2 Exploring social perception

Objectives	Activity	Time (in mins)
To remind group members about what was learnt from the previous session, to give an opportunity to discuss issues or feedback about homework and to set out the aims of the current session	Review the previous session, obtain feedback from homework and set the aims for this session	10
To raise awareness of community life	What are communities?	10
To enable group members to understand the advantages of belonging to different communities	Why live in communities?	15
To promote understanding of how what group members feel about themselves affects how they interact and relate to the community	Self-esteem and communities	20
BREAK		10
To create understanding of how communities work	How communities work	25
To raise awareness of how the communities each person belongs to can both limit and expand their development possibilities	Communities I belong to	20
To check that outcomes have been achieved and explain the homework assignment	Review the session and set homework assignment	5

Positive Interaction Skills

Activity guidelines

Review the previous session, obtain feedback from homework and state the aims of the current session

Reminding people of what they gained from the previous session provides a useful link. Do this by asking each group member to state one thing they learnt from the last session. Complete the exercise by doing a brief summary of their statements.

Next, ask group members how they got on with their homework. Collect in the completed Handout 2 from Session 1. Did anyone have any problems with it? Discuss any issues and help individuals solve problems. Explain that you will keep Handout 2 until the last session of the course, when you will give it back to them.

Hand out your finalised list of the sessions the course will cover and outline the aims and expected learning outcomes for the current session.

What are communities?

Write the word 'COMMUNITY' on a flip-chart. Discuss briefly what the word means using the explanations – taken from the Concise Oxford Dictionary and outlined in Handout 1 – as a starting point.

When ready, have the group brainstorm as many different types of communities as they can think of. These should include religious, political, social, home and any type of situation in which people relate and interact with each other. Some groups or communities may have a short or limited life, may last for many years or a lifetime. Examples are given in Handout 1, which can be distributed at the end of the discussion.

Why live in communities?

Ask group members to brainstorm the advantages of belonging to different communities? Some benefits are listed in Handout 2.

Ask the participants if all communities provide the same benefits or do different communities offer different benefits? Encourage them to state what they have benefited from by belonging to different communities or would like to benefit them. End by giving out Handout 2.

Self-esteem and communities

Have the group discuss the following:

> ★ What is self-esteem? (A definition is provided in Handout 3).
> ★ What roles do the communities individuals belong to play in how they develop self- esteem? (Ensure that the following ideas, listed in Handout 3, are discussed.)
> ★ How is the sense of self-esteem affected by the role people have in the communities to which they belong? Have the group state their feelings from their own experience. (Example statements are provided in Handout 3.)
> ★ What areas of interaction in peoples' lives are affected by their sense of self-esteem? (Example statements are provided in Handout 3.)

Encourage individuals to quote personal experiences of how they have been affected. Round the activity up by asking the group what life would be like without communities? What would be lost? How would it affect them as individuals? End by giving out Handout 3.

How communities work

Form everyone into two groups. Ask one group to imagine that they are going to join a group of people who are going to sail a boat for two weeks. The event has been advertised as an adventure holiday. None of the people have met before. Tell the other group that they have been looking for a job and are joining a large group of workers who have been employed by a big company to help complete a large order of component parts. Everyone will be working in the packaging department to help pack and dispatch the products. There is a possibility that some of the new workers will be offered a permanent contract. Have each group consider:

> ★ What problems might arise?
> ★ What might be a good way to deal with them?
> ★ What interaction skills would they need to ensure a successful outcome and that they had a good experience?
> ★ What are the parallels to the above in any of the communities (groups or families) to which members belong, including the positive interaction group?

Allow time for both groups to draw some conclusions, have each one present their findings to everyone and discuss the points presented.

Communities I belong to

Using Handout 5, have the group members draw in the communities to which they belong at present, as shown in the example in Handout 4. When completed, have a brief discussion on how the communities individuals belong to can limit or expand their development of life possibilities. Do people cope well or have difficulty in some areas?

Complete the activity by getting suggestions about how learners might go about joining other communities and what might stop them. Do people remain part of the same communities because they meet their needs or because they fear trying out other communities?

Review the session and set the homework assignment

Go through the learning outcomes and state what has been achieved. Give group members another copy of Handout 5 and ask them to fill in the communities they want to remain part of in black ink. Then add additional communities they would like to join in blue ink. They can add additional balloons as required. Explain that it is OK to retain all their current communities, if they are happy with them.

Handout 1 What are communities?

A community is:

☆ A group of people living together in one place;

☆ A place considered together with its inhabitants: a rural community, for example;

☆ The people of an area or country considered collectively: a society;

☆ A group of people having a religion, race or profession in common: the scientific community;

☆ The condition of having certain attitudes and interests in common;

☆ Joint ownership or liability.

Examples of communities are:

prayer group	art group
fan club	evening class
job club	football club
swimming group	darts team
school reunion	social club
bowling team	coffee morning
family gatherings	work outing
staff meeting	lunch meeting
going for a meal	going shopping
going to the cinema	work team

Positive Interaction Skills

Handout 2 Benefits of belonging to communities

The benefits of belonging to a community could include:

☆ To form friendships
☆ To have support from other people
☆ To support other people
☆ To have a feeling of belonging
☆ To have a sense of identity
☆ To share a common purpose
☆ For protection and safety
☆ For companionship
☆ To have rights
☆ To have cooperation
☆ To give and receive dignity and respect
☆ To ensure freedom.

Handout 3 Self-esteem and communities (1 of 2)

A definition of self-esteem might be:

☆ Confidence in one's own worth and abilities

The role communities play in how self-esteem is developed includes:

☆ Being responsible for self

☆ Social responsibilities

☆ Respecting social rules

☆ Shared values

☆ Appreciating and valuing other people

☆ Respecting self and other people

☆ Being appreciated and valued by other people

☆ Acceptance by others

☆ Influence in what happens in the communities.

Sense of self-esteem can be affected by the role played in the communities you belong to in the following ways:

☆ Feeling good about yourself

☆ Feeling bad about yourself

☆ Respecting yourself and other people

☆ Poor interaction skills inhibiting ability to develop better self-esteem

☆ Not taking responsibility

☆ Distrust and disrespect for others

☆ Embarrassment.

Handout 3 Self-esteem and communities (2 of 2)

The areas of interactions affected by self-esteem include:

- Family
- Friendships
- Work
- Ability to influence people
- Hobbies and interests
- How you get on in life
- Sex
- Control over what happens to you
- How you feel about yourself and others
- Ability to take part in community life
- How you interact and respond in situations
- Attitude to life
- Learning
- Ability to acquire new skills
- Romance.

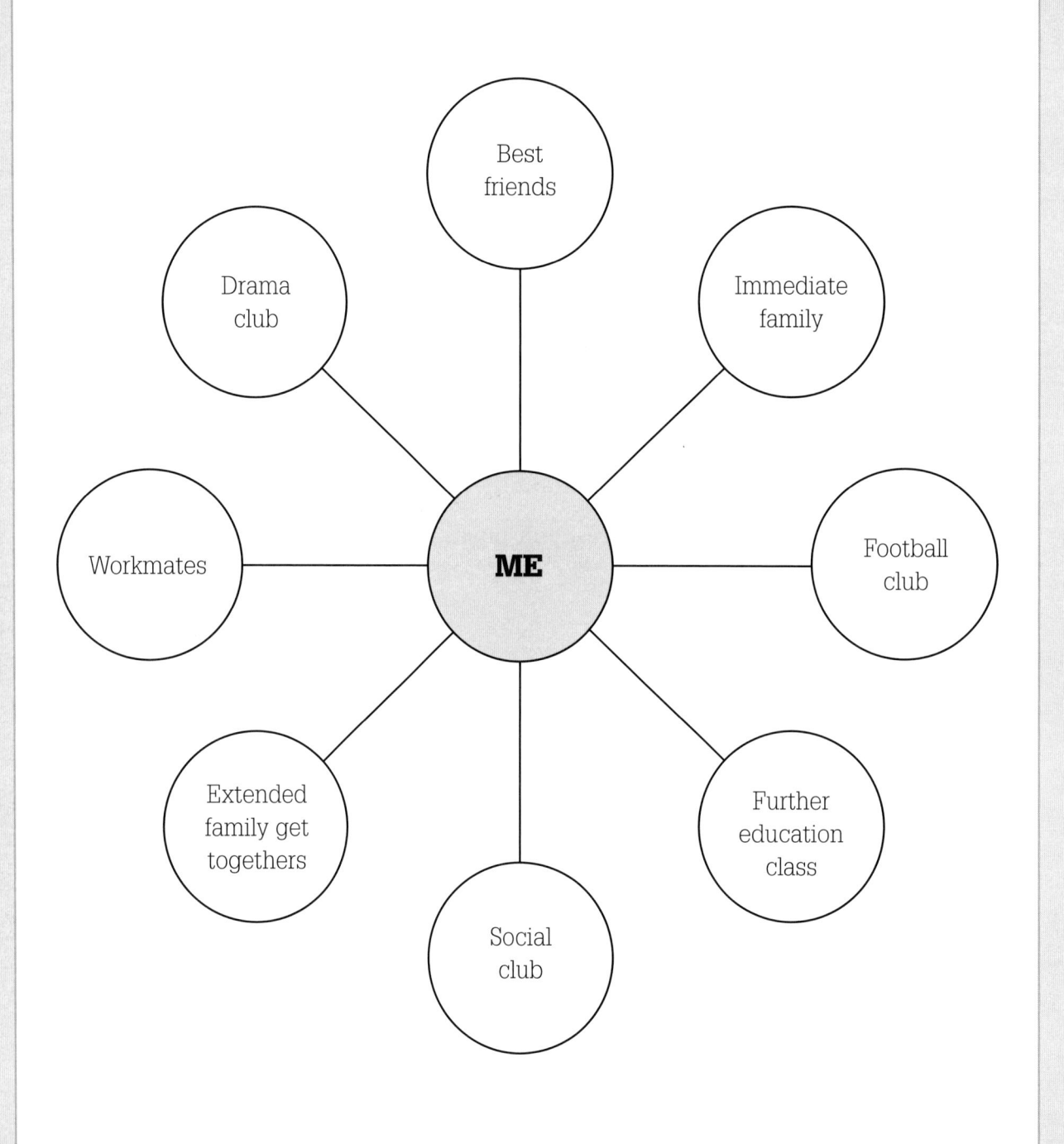

Handout 4 Communities I belong to – example

- Best friends
- Immediate family
- Football club
- Further education class
- Social club
- Extended family get togethers
- Workmates
- Drama club

ME

Handout 5 Communities I belong to

Write a community you belong to in each of the balloons. Write, in a different colour, in any balloons left, any additional communities you would like to belong to. If necessary, draw some extra balloons.

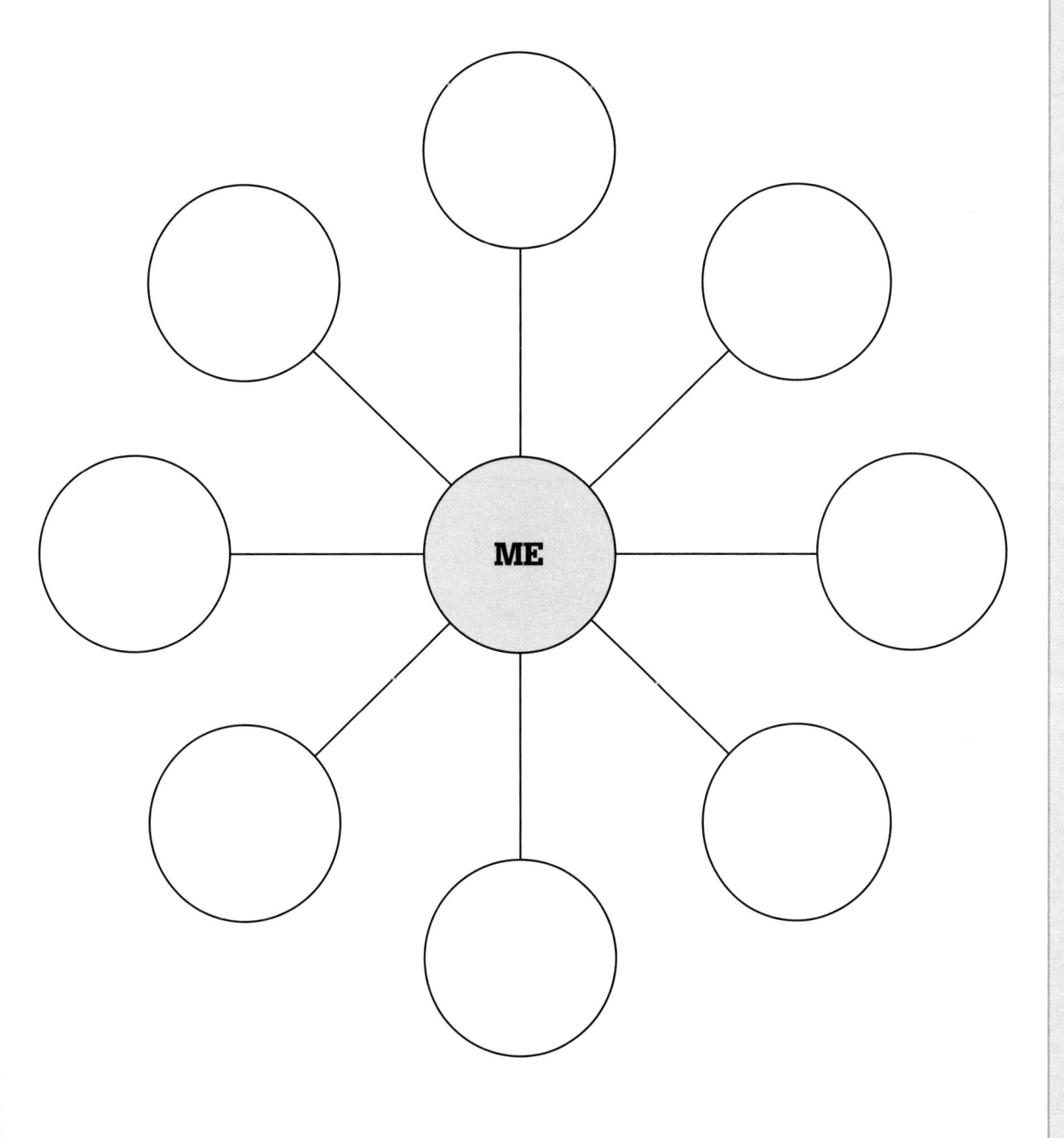

ME

3 Recognising influences on interaction

Aim

To enable group members to recognise what has influenced how they interact and develop relationships.

Learning Objectives

By the end of the session group members will understand:

- How they learn from other people;
- How interaction and relationship behaviour develops;
- How their own interaction and relationship behaviour has developed;
- What personal development is;
- What influences development;
- What has influenced development of their own relationships;
- That they can choose to make changes.

Introduction

Enabling group members to recognise what influences how they interact and develop relationships helps them:

- Be aware of what has influenced their ability to interact;
- How they can change and develop their interaction skills;
- Be aware of the importance of interaction on their personal development;
- Motivate themselves to learn and make changes;
- See the importance of past experiences and self-awareness in the learning process.

Recognising what influences how people interact and what makes them interact in the way they do is a first step in thinking about how they can initiate change. It gives a clear picture of where they are now. This session helps group members to build a picture of how they see themselves interacting at this time in their lives and to start thinking about how they want to be able to interact in the future.

Everyone will have a range of experiences of interacting with others. They may:

- Lack confidence and self-esteem;
- Have all sorts of negative thoughts about failing to communicate their thoughts, feelings and wishes;
- Feel ignored and not valued by others.

The activities are designed to help group members to appreciate the value of experience and how it can be used to learn and make changes.

Can you remember incidences when you tried to communicate and failed? For example, have there been times when you have given up trying to get something across to your line manager, a spouse or a friend? What prevented you? Was it shyness, misunderstanding, fear of what the reaction might be, feeling that you were not important enough for them to pay attention to you, unable to find the right time, them not listening? How did you feel? Ignored, hopelessly isolated with the problem? How did it affect the relationship? What did or would have helped you to stop feeling as you did about yourself? How can you use your experience to help group members to feel better about themselves? What were the behaviour messages you learnt from others which influenced how you dealt with the situation and how your interaction skills have developed?

Preparing to do the activities

What you learn from the people around you

Many things influence how individuals interact and relate to other people. It is helpful to think about what these influences are and to decide if they are helpful or unhelpful. People can then make a choice about whether or not to make changes. This exercise is the first step to achieving that. Read through Handout 1 and think about examples from your own life and the people you know well.

Influences of family and friends

Some group members may find this exercise difficult and will need support. It is not always easy to acknowledge issues that may normally be considered very private or are the cause of embarrassment. Also, bear in mind that some discussion might be necessary about whether or not a behaviour message is negative or positive. These issues are not always black and white. What might be considered positive to one person may be considered negative by someone else in different circumstances. It also needs to be considered in light of what the person wants to achieve and if the message is helpful (or not) in achieving this.

What is personal development?

It is essential that group members have a common understanding of what you mean by personal development before attempting the exercises in this session. It will help them to make the connection with the previous exercise concerning behaviour messages.

Influences on personal development

The behaviour messages learnt from the people around individuals have a strong influence on how they develop. Thinking through the case study examples will prepare group members for the next activity, when they will be looking at the influences on their own development. Group members are likely to arrive with other behaviour messages and their effects, rather than use those listed. The list provided is intended to give examples only.

My personal development

These exercises are not about blaming people who may have provided unhelpful behaviour messages or influenced someone's development in a negative way – they were likely to be doing their best in whatever circumstances they lived. Everyone is responsible for their own life and can choose to change it if they wish to do so.

Again, some group members may find this exercise difficult and may need support to make connections. Also, insight can sometimes be emotional and bring up feelings that are hard to manage, whether it be sadness at something missed out on so far, or a motivating discovery. Facing making changes and the effect that can have on the people around an individual can create very mixed and fearful emotions. Being aware of these feelings from your own experience will help you to support individuals and keep the ending of the session positive.

3 Recognising influences on relationship development

Objectives	Activity	Time (in mins)
To remind group members about what was gained from the previous session, to give an opportunity to discuss issues or feedback about homework and to set out the aims of the current session	Review previous session, obtain feedback from homework and set out aims for this session	10
To make individuals aware of what they learn from the people who surround them	What do you learn from the people around you?	15
To make group members aware of how their personal interaction behaviour has developed	Influences of family and friends	30
BREAK		10
To clarify understanding of what personal development is	What is personal development?	5
To make group members aware of how interaction influences personal development	Influences on personal development	25
To raise group members' awareness of what has influenced their personal development and how negative influences can be changed	My personal development	20
To check that outcomes have been achieved and explain the homework assignment	Review the session and set homework assignment	5

Positive Interaction Skills

3. Activity guidelines

Review previous session, obtain feedback from homework and state the aims of the current session

Summarise briefly the learning points from the previous session. Discuss successes and difficulties with the homework and outline the aim for the current session.

What you learn from the people around you

Explain that how individuals interact and behave in relationships is influenced by the people around them. Everyone needs to look at these influences and decide if the behaviour messages they have picked up are helpful or unhelpful. Give out Handout 1 and go through the areas listed. Encourage group members to give you examples from their own lives for each area.

Influences of family and friends

Give out Handout 2. Go through the two examples given and add other examples if required to aid understanding. Then ask the group members to fill in behaviour messages they have identified for themselves and state if they feel they are helpful or unhelpful. End the activity by asking learners to share behaviour messages and whether or not they feel they are helpful or unhelpful. Discuss.

What is personal development?

Have the group members discuss what they think personal development is and what might hold it back. Ensure that the following points are made. Personal development is:

- How an individual grows and learns to cope with life in a way that suits him/her;
- How people learn to make changes to help them make the most of themselves;
- Individual to each person as to how they grow and develop – each person will have a different ideas about what they want and how to achieve it;
- Getting to know and understand yourself;
- Held back by bad experiences or influences;
- Achieved through choice: individuals can ignore any interaction and relationship problems they have, or work at improving their interaction skills to help them develop better relationships.

Influences on personal development

Divide the members into two groups. Give each group a copy of Handout 3. Ask one group to concentrate on Case Study 1 and the other on Case Study 2. Ask both groups to do two tasks:

> ★ Task 1 Write down the behaviour messages the person in their case study is being given.
>
> ★ Task 2 Write down what effects these have had on the person's personal development.

When both groups have completed their tasks, bring everyone back together again to share their conclusions. End the activity by giving out Handout 4, which contains some example answers.

Point out that influences are seldom all good or all bad – that most people have a combination of both, but that it is how they deal with the influence, once they are aware of it, that is important to personal development. Individuals may also have interpreted an influence in a negative way, that was not intended, or an influence may have been appropriate in the past, but is not now. It is not helpful to try to apportion blame to parents or others for influences.

My personal development

Give out Handout 5. Using the behaviour messages participants wrote down using Handout 2, ask them now to write down – using Handout 5 – the effects that the behaviour messages have had on the development of their interaction skills and relationships. When completed, ask the group members to share their conclusions if they feel able to. End the activity by pointing out that becoming aware of this information about themselves is a big step towards dealing with problems.

Homework

Give out Handout 6 and ask everyone to spend some time during the next week writing down other behaviour messages they become aware of and the effect on their personal development.

Handout 1 Things you learn from people around you

Some of the things you learn from people around you are:

Appearance	How to dress, react when you meet someone, say goodbye. How to look when angry or pleased.
Trust	Whether or not to trust people.
Dealing with conflict	To make compromises, bully the other person, go silent, ignore someone, or threaten them.
Meeting people	What to do when you meet other people socially, at work or in authority.
Self-esteem	How you think other people feel about you. This is influenced by friends, teachers, bosses, family and so on.
What is important	A sense of what is important to friends, family, bosses and so on.
Values	What value is placed on relationships by different people and what they will do for you.
Feelings	How to show what you feel: love disappointment, anger, pleasure, etc.
How to react to others	People who you like, dislike, in authority, those who annoy you, strangers and so on.
Behaviour	How to behave on different occasions, such as when in church, at work, at home or in a friend's house.

Handout 2 Influences of family and friends

Interaction behaviour messages I have learnt from my family and friends are:

Example

Behaviour message	Negative or positive
My parents never spoke for days when they disagreed about something. We lived in tense silence until one of them gave in.	Negative
My aunt and uncle always discussed things with each other and agreed what each of them wanted to do.	Positive

Behaviour message	Negative or positive

Handout 3 Influences on personal development (1 of 2)

Case Study 1

Angela lives with her elderly grandparents. She does all their shopping, looks after them and takes them most places they want to go in her car. She feels she does not have a life of her own, but is afraid to do anything about this. She lacks confidence in herself, thinks nobody likes her or wants anything to do with her.

When young, her grandparents were very critical of anything she did and often compared her unfavourably with other children. They are still critical and Angela thinks she is a failure and disappointment to them and their daughter, who died in a car accident. She was never allowed to go out on her own. She was never allowed to have friends to stay or to stay at friends' houses. Anyone she played with or had as a friend had to be approved by her grandparents and their parents had to be professional people. She did have two friends at college for a short time, but had to be secretive about them.

When growing up, Angela always had to help her grandmother manage the home. Angela thinks that her grandmother resented having to bring her up and blames this as the reason for her ill health. Angela's grandfather was a quiet man who rarely risked disagreeing with his wife. If he did, she became verbally aggressive and sulked for days, refusing to cook or do anything for him. Nor would she allow Angela to do so.

Handout 3 Influences on personal development (2 of 2)

Case Study 2

Peter is a confident man who is successful in his career as a nurse. At work he is thought to be a good manager. He talks things through with his staff and always explains his reasons for doing things and setting boundaries. He is thought to be fair, but expects people to be hard-working and to contribute in a positive way to the team he manages. He enjoys the company of other people, no matter what their background. He lives close to his parents, sees them often and frequently seeks their advice.

When he was growing up, his parents laid down guidelines he had to adhere to – such as times to be in, places he could not go because they were thought to be unsafe and so on. They gave him a lot of praise, encouraged him to set his own goals and to take responsibility for achieving them. They encouraged him to stay with his friends and bring friends to stay with them. They did not mind what background his friends came from as long as they were not rude, didn't steal from them, or were not involved in drugs.

When he did something they did not approve of, they talked it through with him and explored the reasons for their disapproval. If he did something he was forbidden to do, he either had to donate some of his pocket money to a charity or was given tasks to do to benefit the household or other people, depending on what he had done. When he was punished, his parents told him that they still loved him, just disapproved of what he had done.

Handout 4 Messages and effects from the case studies

Case Study 1

Behaviour messages
- If she doesn't do as she is told she will suffer
- She is not to be trusted
- Other people cannot be trusted
- The person's background is most important when making friends
- She has to be secretive to be able to make friends with people she likes

Effects on personal development
- Poor self-esteem
- She feels guilty if she does anything of which her grandparents disapprove
- She fears disapproval, restricting her motivation to make new friends
- As she is constantly undermined, she lacks confidence to become independent
- Lack of independence has not given her enough experience to be assertive

Case Study 2

Behaviour messages
- Most people can be trusted
- Behaviour is more important than background
- It is important to talk things through
- Take responsibility for what you do
- Punishment should fit the crime and benefit other people
- He can be trusted
- It is possible to disapprove of bad behaviour, but still love someone

Effects on personal development
- Good self-esteem
- Feels confident
- He trusts his staff, but sets boundaries
- He lives independently of his parents, but supports and respects them
- He feels he can make his own decisions and live his own life
- He enjoys a good social life and is confident when meeting new people

Handout 5 My personal development

Negative effects that behaviour messages have had on my personal development	Source

Positive effects that behaviour messages have had on my personal development	Source

Handout 6 Behaviour message and development awareness chart

Behaviour message	Effect on personal development	Negative or positive	Source

Session 3: Recognising influences on interaction

4 Developing support networks

Aim

To enable group members to explore, understand and be able to strengthen and develop their support networks and to improve their interaction skills in this process.

Learning Objectives

By the end of the session group members will understand:

- What a support network is and how it works;
- Their own personal networks;
- How support networks change constantly;
- How to strengthen and develop them;
- What benefits they get from their own support network;
- What they give in return;
- What changes they want to make to their support network.

4 Introduction

This session is intended to enable learners to take responsibility for their own support networks and how they use and develop them. Without an adequate support network individuals become isolated and vulnerable. If a realistic and sustainable network is established, it will help enable individuals to make and sustain satisfactory relationships.

It should be reinforced throughout the session that, without reasonable interaction skills, a network is very difficult to maintain. Interaction is at the heart of all relationships and networks whether it is:

- Within the family;
- Friendships;
- At work;
- Having a good social life;
- Marriage;
- Raising a family;
- Communicating with professionals, such as doctors and nurses;
- Dealing with authority;
- Obtaining a job.

It is obvious from the above that interaction skills are essential in all aspects of life.

It will be helpful when preparing for the session to have a comprehensive list of, or leaflets from, local agencies to supply information when individuals identify areas of need in their support networks. Local agencies might include:

- Financial advisory services;
- Adult learning or college brochures;
- Societies to join;
- Relationship guidance services;
- Support groups;
- Job or career advisory services.

Preparing to do the activities

What is a support network?

Everyone needs links with other people for support to cope with a complex world and to meet their everyday needs. Have a look at your own support network – knowing how you are supported and are able to sustain your lifestyle will be invaluable in reinforcing the importance of a support network. It is paramount that you emphasise the need for everyone to take responsibility for their own network and its role in supporting them in achieving their ambitions and sustaining their desired lifestyles.

Identifying your personal support network

Some group members will have more sustained and extensive support networks than others. Some may have difficulty identifying and acknowledging people and agencies who support them. It is necessary to move around the group giving assistance as required. Ask questions like:

- Do you belong to a club? Who do you see and talk to there?
- Do you attend a class? Does the tutor support you in any way?
- Do you meet anyone for a coffee regularly or go to the cinema with anyone?
- Does a nurse or occupational therapist come to see you regularly?

By this stage in the course you will be fairly familiar with each person's background. Use this knowledge to draw out their networks as required.

What changes?

The one constant thing in the modern world is change – sometimes slow, but more often fast. Raising awareness of how events and circumstances can change support networks and of the need to make continuous adjustments to them is essential to maintaining a good, healthy support system.

Look back over some of the changes and adjustments you have made over the past five or 10 years. Did someone important to you move away? Did this leave a gap? What adjustments did you make? Did you form other friendships to replace them? Did you change jobs? What effect did this have on your network over a period of time? Perhaps you had another child. What difference did this make?

Strengthening your network

With your knowledge of the group members, you will probably have built up a good idea of who has and who does not have a reasonable network in the group. When splitting people into small groups or pairs for this activity, make sure that at least one person has a reasonable network. If you put two people together with poor networks they may find it very difficult to provide each other with ideas. There is also a danger of placing someone with a very good network with someone who has a very poor one. Try to avoid this extreme as it could, if the person with the good network reinforced any feelings of inadequacy, have a negative effect.

Also, instruct the group that only positive and constructive comments about other individuals' networks are acceptable.

Giving in return

This can be an enlightening exercise. So often, it is forgotten that both parties should benefit from a relationship. Sometimes people sustain a relationship because it is familiar and both parties have long since ceased to benefit from it. It has just become habit. If so, a decision needs to be made whether or not to maintain it. It may be difficult to know what benefits another person receives from a relationship or what qualities they appreciate. It is probably best to ask. This could be phrased something like: 'I really benefit from talking things through with you. It helps me get them in proportion. What do you get out of our friendship?'

4 Developing support networks

Objectives	Activity	Time (in mins)
To remind group members what was gained from the previous session, to give an opportunity to discuss issues or feedback about homework and set the aims for the current session	**Review previous session, obtain feedback from homework and set out aims for this session**	10
To explore what support networks are, what people get from – and contribute – to them	**What is a support network?**	20
To enable group members to understand their own support network	**Identifying your personal support network**	30
BREAK		10
To raise awareness that support networks are changing constantly	**What changes?**	10
To look at ways individuals can strengthen their networks	**Strengthening your network**	15
To examine what support individuals get from their networks and contribute in return	**Giving in return**	20
To check that outcomes have been achieved and explain the homework assignment	**Review the session and set homework assignment**	5

4 Activity guidelines

Review previous session, obtain feedback from homework and state the aims of the current session

Ask each group member to state one thing they learnt during the last session. Ensure that all the learning points are covered, discuss any points raised and outline the aims for the current session.

Positive Interaction Skills

What is a support network?

Discuss with the group what their understanding of a support network is. A definition that one group thought of is supplied in Handout 1.

When the discussion is completed, ask the group members to call out a list of the types of people they have connections or links with and write them on a flip-chart. Suggestions are supplied in Handout 1. Discuss whether or not some people on the list are more important than others and who these are.

Now, ask why group members should bother to maintain interaction and contact with the people on the list, and discuss. Again, sample answers are given in Handout 1.

Lastly, ask if the group members think that they should give anything back to the people who form their support networks. Discuss why? Suggestions are contained in Handout 1.

Give out Handout 1 to the group members for them to keep.

Identifying your personal support network

Ask each group member to make a list of the people or agencies that form their social network. Suggest they start with family members and work out from there, including friends, work, college and so on. When this is complete, give out Handouts 2 and 3, and have people draw their own support network chart. Request that, when drawing, they place the people who are most important in their network closest to them and the least important further away. Handout 2 gives an example of a chart.

What changes?

Ask the group members if they think that their support network will always be the same, or does it change? Get them to call out ways in which it is likely to change and what might affect it. Examples of things which could affect change are:

- Deciding to make changes;
- Changing jobs;
- Leaving home;
- Getting married;
- Moving away to live in another area;
- Changing college or school;
- Other people moving away or changing jobs;
- A bereavement.

Explain that some changes will be good, whereas others will leave gaps in their support network. Good interaction skills are required to maintain the network needed and to replace the gaps made when events beyond the individual's control happen. Sometimes good changes, like getting married and having children, change what is required in a support network. Thus both good and bad changes bring about the need to adjust individual support networks.

Strengthening your network

Divide the group into sub-groups or pairs, to compare network charts and then discuss with each other how they might strengthen their individual support networks. Ask participants to make only positive suggestions to each other and to ensure that nobody jokes or makes comments about anyone who has a very limited network. Ask people not to alter their charts, but to write notes of possible changes or additions they would like to make.

Giving in return

Remind people that relationships are two-way channels and that they also need to be contributing in some way to that relationship by giving something back. Give out Handout 4. Next, ask the group members to list the people in their support networks and to write down what support they receive from each person and what they contribute in return. If they do not contribute in return for support, then ask them to think about what they could contribute and write that in the space. They should then consider putting this into practice if they want to maintain the support they are receiving.

Homework

Give out another copy of Handout 3 and ask everyone to redraw their support network, this time making it represent how they would like it to be. They may want to change the distance people are away from them, put in additional support or leave other support out. They will then be able to complete Handout 5.

Make it clear to people that they should not try to work on all the changes at once. They should work on them one at a time, starting with the easiest, and then, as they develop more skills during the course, they can gradually begin working on more difficult tasks.

Handout 1 What is a support network?

One definition of a support network is: 'It is all the people and agencies around you with whom you have links and connections and from whom you get support.'

People and agencies you get support from may include:

family members	landlord	workmates
friends	team-mates	community nurses
social workers	tutors	union representative
manager	neighbours	bank manager

and many others.

It is important to interact and maintain contact with these people because the support I get includes:

☆ Financial advice and support
☆ Help when solving problems
☆ Companionship
☆ Someone to talk to when I feel terrible
☆ Being able to share things with them
☆ Having help when I want to do something like decorate my room
☆ Having someone to have fun and relax with
☆ Receiving advice and guidance on how to do tasks.

In return I can give things like:

☆ Help when they need to do their garden
☆ Getting their shopping when they are feeling unwell
☆ Assisting them with their decorating
☆ Taking time to listen to their problems
☆ Helping them when they are stressed or pressured
☆ Using my sense of humour to lighten things up
☆ Keeping my agreements with them.

Handout 2 Example support network chart

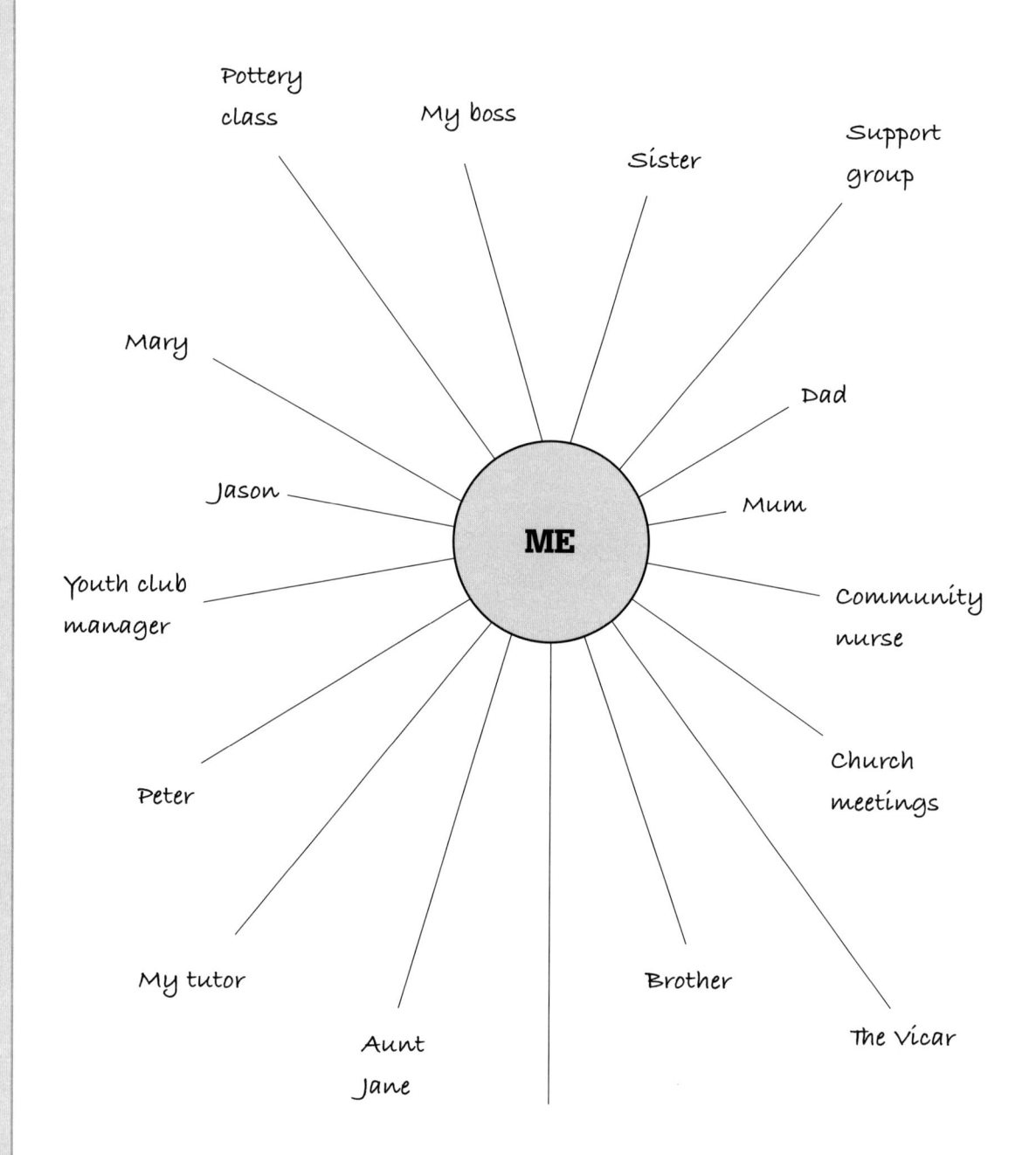

- Pottery class
- My boss
- Sister
- Support group
- Mary
- Dad
- Jason
- Mum
- Youth club manager
- Community nurse
- Peter
- Church meetings
- My tutor
- Brother
- Aunt Jane
- The Vicar
- Landlord

ME

Positive Interaction Skills

Handout 3 Personal support network chart

ME

Handout 4 Giving in return

Name	What benefit I receive	What I give in return

Handout 5 Support network changes

Changes I want to make to my support network are:	What I would like from them is:	What I can offer in return is:

Session 4: Developing support networks

5 Understanding body language

Aim
To enable group members to become aware of what body language is and how it affects how they interact and relate with other people.

Learning Objectives
By the end of the session group members will understand:
- What body language is;
- Its importance in relationships;
- Their own use of body language;
- The difference between good and bad body language;
- Appropriate use of body language in different situations;
- How they can use body language to improve their own interactions.

Introduction

Body language can tell as much about people as anything they might say. Exploring it as a means of communication helps group members to:

- Understand the messages their own body language is giving;
- Read other people's non-verbal communications and respond appropriately;
- Present a more positive image of themselves;
- Develop, with experience, an instinct for recognising expressions, gestures and postures that indicate something meaningful;
- Use their body language to reinforce and compliment what they are trying to say.

As much as 65 percent of what is communicated is said to be shown through body language; that is, through eye contact, body posture, gestures, proximity to other people and facial expression. Gestures, facial expression and how words are spoken are frequently more reliable indicators of what people are feeling than what is actually said. Often this silent language compliments what is being said, reinforcing the words spoken.

The exercises in this session enable group members to begin to explore and develop awareness of what their own body language says about them, either intentionally or unintentionally. In order to interact successfully they also need to know how to 'read' other people's body language.

For example, you could explain that it is possible to watch a couple talking at the far end of a crowded bar, without hearing what they are saying, and, by observing their gestures, postures and proximity to each other, to learn how interested they are in the conversation and even if they are sexually attracted to each other.

To prepare for the session, it is worth spending time observing how you and the people around you use non-verbal communication. Make notes of how your colleagues, friends and family use body language. Switch the television sound off and from your observations interpret what is going on. Be aware how you, yourself, are using gestures, expressions and body language when communicating with others. These are all ways you can heighten your awareness and provide examples for the session.

The type of thing you might note when observing people could include:

- Do they lean forward when showing interest?
- When do they make good eye contact?
- When do they avoid eye contact?
- What gestures do young people make to look grown up – hands in pockets, for instance?
- When does your manager's body language indicate it is not a good time to to raise a particular topic?
- When does body language give a different message to what is being said?
- What body language indicates hostility?
- What are the indicators that people like each other?
- Note the orientation of bodies and feet at a meeting, gathering or party – do people tend to turn towards those they find interesting?
- Is someone peering over the top of their glasses being judgemental?
- Is the person with arms folded putting up a barrier or is it just a comfortable position?
- What indicates that a person is being dominant, arrogant or relaxed?
- What postures indicate that a woman is attracted to a man?
- How does she erect barriers when she is not?
- What postures do men adopt to indicate they are interested in a woman?
- What can you tell from a handshake?
- What postures does a boss adopt?

Do point out to group members that it cannot be assumed that postures and gestures have universal meanings. In some countries, if you beckon a Muslim with an upturned palm, the gesture would be regarded as obscene. In Greece, holding up thumbs to hitch a lift would be thought insulting. Making direct eye contact in some cultures may also be interpreted as rude.

This indicates that not all body language can be read successfully. It can sometimes mean different things to different people, even in different parts of the same country and among people from different cultural backgrounds. Sensitivity and care are needed about this. However, so much can be interpreted successfully that becoming aware of body language will provide group members with a great deal of insight and improve their ability to communicate and interact successfully.

Preparing to do the activities

Without words

This exercise introduces and explains what body language is and starts discussion on what is involved and how important body language is when interacting with other people. Having a go with some of the prepared cards or looking at your own expressions in a mirror will be helpful and give you a feel for the exercise when preparing for the session.

What my body language is saying

When doing this exercise with the group, emphasise the need to match what is being said with what is being communicated through expression, speech and other body language. When these do not match, what is the effect? Might the message be misunderstood? The person listening might think the person speaking is being insincere or sarcastic. Think back to times when incidences like these have occurred to you. How did you feel? What was the effect?

Get out of my space

Some people might feel quite uncomfortable when placed in a situation that imposes on their body space. Be aware and support anyone who has difficulty doing the exercise. Think back to a time when somebody invaded your space and how uncomfortable it felt, or what the effect was when someone stood too far away from you when having a conversation. What was communicated to you and how did you feel? How did it affect your impression of that person?

Look me in the eye

This is a powerful exercise that demonstrates the effect of disinterest in a person and the difference appropriate body language can make when interacting with others.

How do I look?

Being dressed inappropriately can create an immediate effect on a situation. How have you felt when you have turned up to an event and found that you had misjudged the occasion and the appropriateness of appearance? How have you felt about someone else who inadvertently did the same or who turned up either not caring or unaware of the effect their appearance had?

5 Understanding body language

Objectives	Activity	Time (in mins)
To remind the group members of what was gained from the previous session, to give opportunity to discuss issues or feedback about homework and to set aims for the current session	**Review previous session, obtain feedback from homework and set out aims for this session**	10
To introduce and explain what body language is and its importance in relationships	**Without words**	20
To explore the use of gesture, posture and manner of speech	**What my body language is saying**	20
To experiment with the use of personal space	**Get out of my space**	15
BREAK		10
To experience both good and bad eye contact	**Look me in the eye**	25
To explore the effects of personal appearance on interactions	**How do I look?**	15
To check that outcomes have been achieved and explain the homework assignment	**Review the session and set homework assignment**	5

5 Activity guidelines

Review previous session, obtain feedback from homework and state the aims of the current session

Write 'One thing I learnt in the last session was …' on a flip-chart and ask each group member to call out a learning point from the previous session, then write them up on the chart. Discuss successes and difficulties with the homework. Keep this exercise brief and to the point. Next, outline the aims for the current session.

Without words

Prepare a set of cards with a different feeling or emotion written on each one. These feelings might be:

happy	nervous	guilty
sad	irritated	surprised
anxious	frightened	relaxed
angry	bored	confident
pleased	tired	shocked

Give each person in the group a card and ask them – in turn – to express the feeling on their card non-verbally. See if the other group members can guess the feelings being expressed by each person. Once everyone has had a turn, discuss how they recognised the emotions expressed. Write on the flip-chart what the group members say helped them to decide what the emotions were.

This list should include:

- Expression
- Posture
- Gesture
- Eye-contact
- Use of space

Explain to the group members that they have been describing body language – also referred to as 'non-verbal communication'. Now have the group discuss:

- What body language tells them about other people;
- What it tells other people about them;
- The effect when what people say does not match what is shown through their body language;
- How important they think body language is when communicating with other people.

What my body language is saying

Ask group members to choose a partner. Now give each person a slip of paper with one of the following written on it:

confidently	disinterested	disgusted	caring
distrustfully	friendly	bossy	pleased
sarcastically	thoughtfully	abruptly	rudely
coldly	threateningly	defensively	

Positive Interaction Skills

Instruct members not to say what is written on their piece of paper. Now ask each person to have a short conversation with their partner acting in the manner of the word they have been given. Give a moment for thought and have them begin. After a few moments, stop the conversations and bring everyone back into a circle. Now discuss:

> ★ How each person felt;
> ★ What made them feel they way they did;
> ★ What can be added to the list started in the previous exercise. (This should now include tone of voice, pitch, manner in which statements are made, and so on.)

Get out of my space

Here is a list of types of relationships and situations:

> ★ Good friends of the same sex chatting at a party;
> ★ Friends of the opposite sex on a bus together;
> ★ A married couple out for an evening stroll;
> ★ An employer instructing an employee;
> ★ Two people being introduced;
> ★ A boss congratulating someone;
> ★ Friends angry with each other;
> ★ Two friends, one of whom is upset;
> ★ A bully trying to intimidate someone;
> ★ An employee being interviewed;
> ★ Two people out on a date.

Taking a few of the situations, one at a time, choose two group members and place them in what might be inappropriate positions for the situation. For example, two friends of the same sex chatting at a party could have their arms round each other or sprawled out with their feet on chairs. Now ask the two participants how they feel in that position – have them state why and position themselves in a way they feel comfortable. Ask other group members what they feel would be comfortable for them.

Having experimented with one or two situations, have the group discuss others. Ensure that the discussion includes:

- How close they should be physically;
- The type of touching that is acceptable in the situation;
- When touch and being close is appropriate;
- What parts of the body can be touched and by whom;
- What it feels like when someone is too close or too far away;
- What happens when people do not abide by these guidelines.

Look me in the eye

Divide the group into two smaller, equal-numbered groups. Separate them and call one Group A and the other Group B. Speak to those in Group A (so that those in Group B cannot overhear) and tell them that you want them to sit or stand somewhere in the room and that they will be approached by someone from Group B to have a conversation. Instruct them to make eye contact at first and then gradually to start glancing away from the person speaking to them until they are looking out of the window or in another direction for most of the time and to display body language that shows disinterest. Now talk to those in Group B and ask them to approach someone from Group A and talk to them in a friendly and interested manner.

After a few minutes, stop the proceedings. Bring everyone together and discuss how both groups A and B felt. What made it difficult to keep the conversation going?

How do I look?

Below are listed some types of dress and situations. In each case, discuss with the group the appropriateness of one to another. Ensure that the effect of dress to situation, on others as well as to the person experiencing the event, is discussed.

jeans	job interview
suit	working in a carpentry workshop
old dirty clothes	going to a funeral
smart jacket	working as a mechanic
T-shirt and casual shorts	hospital reception
Low-cut evening dress	church

Ask the group members to discuss any occasions when they may have misjudged what they have worn to events and how it made both them and others feel. Finish by exchanging ideas on how people can ensure that their appearance is appropriate to situations.

Homework

Give out Handout 1 and ask the group members to rate themselves on their use of body language – they can discuss various points with friends or other group members to compare their rating with how others see them. Emphasise the importance of them deciding what they can improve on and how they are going to achieve this improvement.

Handout 1 Body language check

Rate yourself on your appropriate use of the following: (remember, body language should match the meaning of what you say)

Rate your abilities in the following areas:	Poor				Good
Facial expression	1	2	3	4	5
Gestures and use of whole body	1	2	3	4	5
Body space	1	2	3	4	5
Eye contact	1	2	3	4	5
Tone of voice	1	2	3	4	5
Personal presentation	1	2	3	4	5

The areas I can improve are:

I will do this by:

6 Making conversation

Aim
To explore basic guidelines for making conversation in different situations.

Learning Objectives
By the end of the session group members will understand:

- What to talk about and what not to talk about in different situations;
- Methods to help prepare themselves to make conversation;
- How to start a conversation, keep it going and end it;
- How to control the flow of conversation.

6 Introduction

It is likely that from time to time you have been in a situation when conversation has been difficult or has ground to a halt leaving an embarrassing silence. So you have some idea of how uncomfortable it can be for someone who is struggling to make conversation or who does not know what to say in a situation.

Explain to the group members that it is possible to avoid this discomfort by improving their conversation skills. Feeling comfortable when having a conversation will improve how everyone feels about themselves. People who are good at conversation are popular, good to have as friends and are a joy to be with. They are also:

- Well informed;
- Effective at making people around them feel special;
- Sensitive to other people;
- Confident and enthusiastic;
- Good at listening.

Conversation skills come more easily to some people than to others. If someone is not naturally good at conversation, there are skills that they can learn to make conversation easier.

When preparing for the session, try some of the activities yourself and reflect on what you learn from doing this. You will be able to add to the suggestions outlined.

Preparing to do the activities

Having something to say

Can you think of ways you have used to prepare yourself for conversations on different occasions? It is likely that you do certain things automatically in an unconscious way. This may be things like:

- Reminding yourself about recent events in the other person's life you can mention.
- Noting in your mind that their mother was ill the last time you met – you must ask how she is.
- The person you are meeting has had a promotion at work – you must congratulate her and ask how she is coping with her new responsibilities.
- Happenings that you want to tell the other person about because you think they will be interested. This may include anything from something about a mutual acquaintance to a good book you have read or a film you have seen and so on.
- Telling them about something you have achieved or a problem you have that they might be able to help you with.

Thinking about conversation

Reflect on some similar situations you have experienced. What did you learn from them? How did you manage the situation? What was the appropriate greeting when you met, given the circumstances – a handshake, a hug or a kiss? How did you start the conversation, keep it going and end it appropriately?

Having a conversation

A good way to prepare yourself for this is to plan a conversation with someone you are meeting and then to reflect on it afterwards. What went as you anticipated? What did not? Were there any surprises? Can you use any examples from the experience as learning points for the session?

Learning from experience

Doing this exercise yourself will provide you with additional ideas from your own experience to add to the lists. It will also help you to reflect on further examples from your own experience that will be useful for the session.

Homework

The homework is important in enabling group members to put what they are learning into practice in their daily lives. Trying this out will make you aware of some of their feelings when doing this and perhaps make you more aware of your own skills.

6 Making conversation

Objectives	Activity	Time (in mins)
To remind group members about what was learnt in the previous session, to give an opportunity to discuss issues or feedback about homework and to set aims of the current session	**Review previous session, obtain feedback from homework and set out aims for this session**	10
To discuss and provide guidelines to help group members to prepare for making conversation	**Having something to say**	15
To explore how to begin, carry on and end a conversation	**Thinking about conversation**	30
BREAK		10
To practise beginning, carrying on and ending a conversation	**Having a conversation**	35
To take stock of what makes a good or bad conversation	**Learning from experience**	15
To check that outcomes have been achieved and to explain the homework assignment	**Review the session and set homework assignment**	5

6 Activity guidelines

Review the previous session, obtain feedback from the homework and state the aims of the current session

Ask group members to state something that they learnt in the last session and have put into practice. Write the learning points on a flip-chart. Discuss successes and difficulties with the homework and outline the aims for the current session.

Having something to say

Write the following situation headings up on a white-board or on different flip-chart sheets:

> * General social event (with strangers or people not well known);
> * A private party with friends;
> * Meeting with work or school friends;
> * Close friends or family members' gathering.

Now ask the group members to call out different ways that they could ensure they had something interesting to talk about in these situations and write the comments up under the appropriate heading. Some of the methods will be common to each heading. Sample answers are provided in Handout 1 which can be given out at the end of the activity.

Thinking about conversation

Write the following situations on separate pieces of paper:

> * Making conversation with someone you know well when you meet them in a supermarket.
> * Making conversation with a stranger you will be working with in the near future.
> * Making conversation with someone you have just met at a party.
> * Talking to your boss in the canteen at lunch.
> * Talking to a family friend you have met unexpectedly.
> * Talking to someone of the opposite sex you would like to invite out when you are not sure if they like you.

Split the group members into pairs. Give each person a copy of Handout 2 and a situation. Now ask them to use the handout sheet to discuss a possible future conversation noting down their comments. Allow about 15 minutes for this and then ask each group to give feedback.

Having a conversation

Pair the group members up with different partners and instruct them to have the conversations previously planned with their new partners. One tells their partner their situation and has the conversation, then the other person takes their turn. Limit the time of each conversation to about five minutes. When this exercise is completed have an open discussion with the group members about their feelings when having the conversation and what they would now add to their previous comments when thinking about the conversation.

Learning from experience

Ask the group to answer the questions listed below. They can call out their ideas as a large group. Sample answers are provided in Handout 3, which can be given out at the end of the activity.

> ★ Why is being good at making conversation important?
> ★ What helps create a good conversation?
> ★ What contributes to a bad conversation?

Homework

Give out Handout 4 and ask group members to rate themselves on their conversation abilities. They can use their notes and Handout 3 to help them do this. They can also discuss various points with friends or other group members to compare their ratings and learn how others see them. It is important that they pick up on points to improve and how they can do this.

Handout 1 Having something to say

Methods of having something to say at different events include the following:

General social events

Updating on current events by reading newspapers and watching the news on television. This should include browsing through the sports, books, films, theatre and other events as well as the news. When doing this, ask yourself questions such as:

- Was the right film star given an award?
- Should that prison conviction have been overruled by the appeal court?
- Does what the politician did warrant his resignation?
- Should Britain have become involved militarily in the latest trouble spot?

Asking yourself questions in this manner will help you to form an opinion on issues so that you can have meaningful discussions about them. Make sure that you find out about local events and issues as well as national events.

Private party with friends

As well as doing the above, write down the names of people whom you know will be at the party and think about what each person is interested in. This may be a sport, art or a particular hobby. These can then be borne in mind when browsing newspapers, the news and so on.

Meeting with work/school/college friends

If making light conversation, any of the above may be appropriate depending on the situation. Other topics you can update yourself on include what is happening in the workplace, college, work or college newsletter. What are the interests of each friend? What events have happened, or are planned for the future, that would be of interest to each person? How are they getting on with their study or project? What are their opinions on issues?

Close friends or family gathering

Here, additional sources of information for conversation might include how the person is getting on at work or college. Also enquire about mutual friends, health, personal relationships and interests.

Handout 2 Thinking about making a conversation

Use the following guide to think about a conversation you are going to have.

- ☆ How can you prepare yourself to have something to talk about?
- ☆ How will you start the conversation?
- ☆ What can you talk about?
- ☆ How can you keep the conversation going?
- ☆ How can you end the conversation?
- ☆ How will you use pauses?
- ☆ What will not be appropriate to talk about or say?
- ☆ How will you make sure the conversation is balanced?
- ☆ What gestures or facial expressions will it be appropriate to use?
- ☆ How much eye contact should you make?
- ☆ How should you use the pitch or tone of your voice?

Handout 3 Learning from experience (1 of 2)

Why is being good at conversation important?

★ It helps when getting to know other people;
★ It allows other people to get to know you;
★ It allows you to express opinions and to listen to other people's opinions;
★ It makes life interesting;
★ It helps to make the right connections;
★ It makes you feel good about yourself;
★ It enables you to find out about things;
★ It enables you to share ideas and information;
★ It helps you to enjoy other company;
★ It enables you to tell other people what you want;
★ It helps you to understand what other people want;
★ It helps you to make good relationships;
★ It makes people feel special;
★ It boosts self-esteem.

What helps to create a good conversation?

★ Listening to the other person;
★ Accepting that other people have different viewpoints;
★ Showing interest in what the other person is saying;
★ Being sincere;
★ Asking open-ended questions;
★ Appropriate body language;
★ Appropriate use of body space;
★ Not using excessive gestures;
★ Keeping up with current events;
★ Not interrupting;
★ Taking turns when speaking;
★ Not going on and on about something;
★ Expressing views in a way that is not hostile or defensive and listening to opposing views;
★ Making good eye contact.

Handout 3 Learning from experience (2 of 2)

What contributes to a bad conversation?

☆ Not listening to other viewpoints;
☆ Not caring what is said;
☆ Not paying attention;
☆ Being distracted;
☆ Not asking questions or asking closed questions;
☆ Maintaining a blank or disinterested expression;
☆ Just talking about yourself;
☆ Constantly interrupting;
☆ Invading the other person's body space or standing too far away;
☆ Looking away all the time;
☆ Not indicating that you understand what is being said;
☆ Not asking for explanations of what you do not understand;
☆ Not meaning what you say;
☆ Not allowing the other person their turn to speak.

Handout 4 Conversation checklist

Reflect on some of the conversations you have during the week, rate yourself and look for areas you can improve.

Rate your abilities in the following areas:	Poor				Good
Being prepared for the conversation	1	2	3	4	5
Starting the conversation	1	2	3	4	5
Keeping the conversation going	1	2	3	4	5
Ending the conversation	1	2	3	4	5
Body language	1	2	3	4	5

The areas I can improve are:

I will do this by:

Session 6: Making conversation

7 Learning to listen

Aim

To enable group members to develop active listening skills.

Learning Objectives

By the end of the session group members will understand:

☆ What active listening means;

☆ Ways to use body language to indicate that they are listening;

☆ Methods of sending positive voice messages to show they are listening;

☆ How to use door openers to aid interaction;

☆ The skill of using reflective skills to convey understanding;

☆ That silences can be used in a positive way;

☆ How to listen in an empathetic way.

7 Introduction

Listening takes up more of people's time when they are awake than any other activity. Most people spend about 30 percent of their time talking and 45 percent listening. (Ralph G Nichols and Leonard A Stevens, *Are you Listening*, McGraw-Hill, New York, 1957). Most of what everyone does in life is influenced by their listening skills or lack of them. This includes:

☆ Friendships
☆ Family relationships
☆ Work relationships
☆ Social activities
☆ Learning
☆ Communicating with customers or clients
☆ Taking instructions about how to do something.

The list is endless, emphasising the importance of listening as a social skill. Unfortunately, researchers claim that about 75 percent of oral communication is lost – either ignored, misunderstood or forgotten.

Think about the times the following have happened to you:

- ★ Have you been interrupted in the middle of something important you were saying?
- ★ Did someone give you advice instead of listening?
- ★ Did someone ignore what you were saying?
- ★ Has someone faked understanding of what you said?
- ★ Has background noise made listening impossible?
- ★ Have feelings you have expressed been ignored?
- ★ Did someone assume they knew how you felt?

What are the other blocks you have experienced?

Now think about good or interesting conversations you have had. What listening skills contributed to making them?

- ★ Was there good eye contact?
- ★ Did the other person show understanding of your viewpoint, although you may not have agreed with each other?
- ★ Were you both sincere in what you said?
- ★ Did each of you check your understanding of what was being said and felt?
- ★ What sort of questions did you ask each other?

Thinking in this way will give you examples to use when explaining concepts in this session.

Preparing to do the activities

Defining 'active listening'

It is very important that the group members understand what 'listening' means. It is not just hearing, but responding to body language as well as to what is spoken. Be aware of your own body language and what it is saying when you are listening. When going through the handout, ask the group members to think of instances when they felt they were being listened to – what did the other person do to make them feel that way?

Techniques for active listening

Try doing this exercise yourself and see what techniques you can think of that are not in Handout 2. Think back to satisfying conversations and picture in your mind what each of you did to make them successful. When doing the exercise with the group, ensure that terms such 'open-ended questions' and 'challenge inconsistencies' are understood.

Learning to listen

The more appropriate the role play situations are to the group members, the more effective this exercise will be. Choose situations that are relevant to individuals' lives. If the situations outlined do not do this, make up situations of your own that are relevant and that fit the life experiences of the group members.

Awareness check

If there is time, this exercise can help to make people aware of some of the things that have a negative effect – it can be helpful to spend a few minutes discussing with the group the effects these have. Prepare by thinking through times when you were trying to get someone to listen and the actions that were displayed which indicated you were not being listened to or were being ignored.

7 Learning to listen

Objectives	Activity	Time (in mins)
To remind group members about what was learnt in the previous session, to give an opportunity to discuss issues or feedback about homework and to set aims for the current session	**Review previous session, obtain feedback from homework and set out aims for this session**	10
To explore the meaning of 'active listening'	**Defining 'active listening'**	15
To discuss different methods of listening in an active way	**Techniques for active listening**	30
BREAK		10
To practise using active listening skills	**Learning to listen**	35
To reinforce learning	**Awareness check**	15
To check what has been achieved and to explain the homework assignment	**Review the session and set homework assignment**	5

Positive Interaction Skills

Activity guidelines

Review the previous session, obtain feedback from homework and state the aims of the current session

Ask group members to share with the group a skill they have thought about and planned to improve from the previous session. Discuss any points raised and outline the aims for the current session.

Defining 'active listening'

Ask the group members what happens when they are trying to converse with someone who does not listen. Next, discuss the difference between 'active listening' and 'passive listening'. Explain that in active listening the listener not only hears what is being said, but also tries to understand what the person who is speaking is feeling. Give out Handout 1, go through it and discuss.

Techniques for 'active listening'

Write the following headings up on a board or flip-chart, one at a time, and ask the group members to call out actions they could do under each heading. (See Handout 2 for examples.)

- Hearing
- Paying attention
- Giving encouragement
- Acknowledging and responding

Give out Handout 2 when the exercise is completed. There will be additional ideas that group members have thought of which can be added to the lists.

Learning to listen

Divide the group members into pairs. Nominate partners as A and B. Assign role-play situations, such as those listed below, to partner A. Have the role written on a slip of paper to give them. A then plays the designated role and B practises using active listening skills. Stop them after a few minutes and give B a role to play. A now practises using active listening skills. After a few minutes stop the role play and bring everyone together again as a group. Have each pair, in turn, give feedback on how the role play felt, what worked and what did not. Was their partner a good listener? What helped the other person to open up? Who felt awkward or comfortable? Why?

Role play situations:

> ★ You are concerned that your best friend has been drinking too much;
> ★ Your parents/son/daughter have decided to get a divorce;
> ★ You have been caught shop-lifting;
> ★ You think your husband/wife/boyfriend/girlfriend has been cheating on you;
> ★ You are worried that you will not have enough money to pay your rent/mortgage/a debt at the end of the month;
> ★ You are not coping very well at work/school/college or a course and don't know whether to give it up or not;
> ★ You think a friend or colleague has told your boss that you are responsible for a mistake that they made;
> ★ You are moaning because you think the holiday you have gone on with your best friend is boring;
> ★ You have changed jobs and think you have made a mistake;
> ★ You don't know who to vote for in an election;

Awareness check

Give out Handout 3 and ask the group members to complete the check. After a set time, go through the handout and compare answers given. If time is limited, just call out each item and let the group members shout out the answers. If there is plenty of time, discuss some of the items.

Homework

Give out Handout 4 and ask the group members to rate themselves and to identify areas to work on during the week when they are engaged in conversations.

Handout 1 Defining 'active listening'

In order to 'actively listen' to someone you need to:

- Be able to hear what the other person is saying;
- Pay attention to what is being said;
- Encourage the other person to keep talking;
- Acknowledge and respond to what is said.

What is the difference between 'hearing' and 'listening'?

'Hearing' is the ability to be aware of and hear sound. 'Listening' involves not just 'hearing' but also:

- Understanding the meaning of what is being said;
- Showing that it is understood;
- If necessary, clarifying that understanding.

Thus, 'listening' involves encouraging others to continue speaking while enabling you to understand what is being said.

Why develop listening skills?

Listening skills help:

- To keep the conversation going;
- With understanding other viewpoints;
- With sharing thoughts and feelings;
- With finding out what others are feeling;
- The other person to disclose personal information;
- To build trust;
- With forming relationships;
- To show respect and concern.

Handout 2 Active listening techniques (1 of 2)

Hearing

☆ Turn off the radio or television;
☆ Make sure only one person speaks at a time;
☆ Speak clearly, using appropriate volume and pitch;
☆ Make sure the other person can see your face;
☆ If noise is making it difficult to hear, move to a quieter area;
☆ If privacy is needed, go somewhere private;
☆ Don't talk too fast.

Paying attention

☆ Face your body towards the person;
☆ Lean forward slightly;
☆ Keep quiet while the other person is speaking;
☆ Make good eye contact;
☆ Have a friendly facial expression.

Giving encouragement

☆ Ask questions – one at a time;
☆ Use short phrases, such as 'I see …', 'Really …', 'For instance …' 'And …', 'Tell me more…', 'What did you do?'
☆ Maintain a friendly, sympathetic but appropriate expression for the situation (smiling may not always be appropriate);
☆ Maintain appropriate body space;
☆ Touch (arm, hold a hand) as appropriate;
☆ Use head nods;
☆ Take turns to talk;
☆ Use facial expression;
☆ Use gestures (but avoid being excessive with them).

Handout 2 Active listening techniques (2 of 2)

Acknowledging and responding

☆ Restate in your own words what you have heard ('You're saying that …', 'What I'm hearing is …', 'Let me see if I understand that …').

☆ State your perception of the other person's feelings ('You seem angry about …', 'You seem really pleased …', 'You're offended by …').

☆ Check what you don't understand ('Do I understand correctly?', 'Can you explain that again?').

☆ Challenge inconsistencies ('You say it is OK, but you seem upset.' 'The last time we spoke you said he was really nice. Now you say you can't stand him.').

☆ Ask questions that follow on.

☆ Use open-ended questions to get the person to expand on what they are saying.

☆ Ask for specific details ('When did this happen?', 'Describe what she did?', 'Why is this so important to you?', 'Have you thought through your options?', 'What do you intend to do?').

Handout 3 Active listening awareness checklist

To become more aware of your listening skills, go through the following checklist. Write 'yes' against those statements that you think help to create a good reaction from others and 'no' against those that hinder a positive reaction when making conversation.

- [ ] Switching the television off
- [ ] Gazing out of a window
- [ ] Sighing
- [ ] Constantly grinning
- [ ] Saying things like 'Tell me more', 'What did you like about it?'
- [ ] Nodding your head
- [ ] Keeping looking at your watch
- [ ] Leaning slightly forward
- [ ] Looking sceptical
- [ ] Folding your arms
- [ ] Staring at the person
- [ ] Asking open-ended questions
- [ ] Keeping quiet when the other person is speaking
- [ ] Playing with a pen
- [ ] Slumping in your chair
- [ ] Fidgeting
- [ ] Turning the radio on
- [ ] Asking for specific details about something
- [ ] Summarising your understanding of what you have heard
- [ ] Asking questions about what you did not understand
- [ ] Talking quickly
- [ ] Talking in a loud voice
- [ ] Asking a lot of questions
- [ ] Drumming your fingers on a table
- [ ] Interrupting what the person is saying
- [ ] Asking the person how they feel
- [ ] Bouncing your foot up and down
- [ ] Changing the topic
- [ ] Blaming the other person ('It's your own fault')
- [ ] Denying the other person's feelings ('You're just feeling sorry for yourself')

Handout 4 Active listening checklist

Rate your skills in the following active listening skills areas. Look for areas to improve.

Rate your abilities in the following areas:	Poor				Good
Hearing	1	2	3	4	5
Paying attention	1	2	3	4	5
Giving encouragement	1	2	3	4	5
Acknowledging and responding	1	2	3	4	5

The areas I can improve are:

I will do this by:

8. Starting, sustaining and ending friendships

Aim
To develop understanding about what friendships are and how relationships start, are sustained and end.

Learning Objectives
By the end of the session group members will understand:

★ What being a friend means;

★ What can be gained from friendships;

★ What encourages friendships;

★ What stops friendships from developing;

★ How to start friendships;

★ How friendships can change;

★ How to sustain valued friendships;

★ How to deal with the ending of friendships.

Introduction

Once individuals are aware of the process of how friendships are formed, what values are placed on them, what affects them, and how best to deal with the ending of friendships, they are better able to have a positive approach to interacting with others and to sustaining relationships. Hindering elements can be minimised to ensure a rewarding experience. This is a first step to improving relationships and interactions at home, work or when involved with leisure activities.

It will help you to go through the activities planned and reflect on your own experience of forming, sustaining and ending relationships.

★ What has hindered relationships?

★ What has helped?

★ What did you want from a particular relationship?

★ How did some of your friendships start?

★ What kept them going?

★ How did some of them end – what would have made the ending more satisfactory?

Preparing to do the activities

What are friends?

It is important that all members of the group reflect on what they want from a friendship – how they can contribute to the friendship and what negative attributes they have that can influence how rewarding it might be. As group facilitator, reflecting back on good and poor relationships you have had will highlight just how important this activity is and give you valuable insight. The activity can be completed as described or, if you can provide extra time, it is helpful to get group members to reflect back on their own experience for examples they can share with the group.

Starting friendships

Think back to your own friendships. How did they start and develop? Think of the life experience of the group members: their backgrounds, work, home life, leisure activities and what opportunities will they be able to take advantage of to start friendships.

Sustaining friendships

Again, reflecting on how you have maintained some of your friendships will help. Most relationships have periods when you feel closer to the other person than at other times. Think about the reasons behind the good and less good times – what events influenced this? How did you manage to keep friendships through the bad times? How could you have sustained a friendship lost during the bad times? Ensure that group members understand the effect different events may have on valued friendships.

When friendships end

It can be very difficult dealing with the end of relationships. There is a sense of sadness and loss – especially when it is a close friend or valued work colleague. Reflect on your own feelings when you had to say goodbye to friends. How did speaking to the person, having a farewell do or a wishing-them-well drink, help with the process?

This exercise can sometimes trigger sad feelings in group members, particularly if someone has had a friendship that has recently ended. So ensure that this exercise is kept positive and that you explore ways in which people can keep in touch, or, if contact has been lost, how it can be made again. Modern technology makes most things possible.

8. Starting, sustaining and ending friendships

Objectives	Activity	Time (in mins)
To remind the group members about what was learnt in the previous session, to give opportunity to discuss issues or feedback about homework and to set aims for the current session	**Review previous session, obtain feedback from homework and set aims for this session**	10
To explore perceptions and expectations of friendships	**What are friends?**	30
To investigate how friendships begin	**Starting friendships**	20
BREAK		10
To examine how friendships are maintained	**Sustaining friendships**	25
To look at positive ways of dealing with the end of a friendship	**When friendships end**	20
To check that outcomes have been achieved and to explain the homework assignment	**Review the session and set homework assignment**	5

8. Activity guidelines

Review previous session, obtain feedback from the homework and state the aims of the current session

Ask group members in turn to state briefly a skill they are working on from the previous session. Discuss any points raised and outline the aims for the current session.

What are friends?

Divide the group into four subgroups, numbering them groups 1, 2, 3 and 4. Give each group a magic marker and a large sheet of paper. Ask Group 1 to write down all the qualities they value in a friend; Group 2 should write down what qualities a friend might value in them; Group 3 are to produce a list of characteristics they do not like in friends, and Group 4 should write down what they get out of friendships. When this exercise has been completed, ask one person from each group to present their findings to everyone.

Clarify that, in order to be a friend and to have friends, it is necessary to have some of the qualities presented by Groups 1 and 2, and to avoid the characteristics listed by Group 3. Ask all the group members to shout out who they think can be friends. Suggestions could include: parents, work colleagues, neighbours, grandparents, tutors, relatives, classmates and so on. Conclude the exercise by handing out and having each person complete Handout 1.

Starting friendships

Ask the group members to suggest different ways that they can meet and make friends with others. Write the suggestions on a chalkboard and discuss. Some suggestions are given in Handout 2, which can be distributed at the end of the activity.

When enough ideas appropriate to the group members' backgrounds have been explored, hold a general discussion on how this initial action can lead to forming a friendship. Also discuss any fears that people might have about initiating the first step.

Sustaining friendships

Explain that, once formed, friendships can change and that this is natural. Ask group members to suggest reasons why relationships change. (Suggestions are given in Handout 3, which can be distributed at the end of the activity.)

Point out that if a person places a value on a relationship, they need to look at ways of sustaining it. Ask group members to give examples from their own experience. (Suggestions are given in Handout 3.)

When friendships end

Friendships come to an end for many reasons. These can include:

- ★ The friendship is no longer valued;
- ★ Moving to a different area;
- ★ No longer having common interests;
- ★ The values of one individual may change;
- ★ Changing jobs.

Give out Handout 4. Ask the group members to look back on their own experiences and to write down why some of their friendships have ended and how they felt about this. When they have done this, ask for some of the reasons. Next, ask if anyone would mind sharing with the group an unsatisfactory experience and then discuss what would have been a better ending to a situation and how this could have been achieved. End by getting each group member to write a list of good ways to end a relationship and then ask them to share their ideas with each other. This list could include:

- Meeting the other person and saying goodbye;
- Wishing the person well;
- Agreeing to phone and meet occasionally;
- Sorting out any disagreements before parting;
- Having a farewell meal together.

Emphasise throughout this activity the importance of saying goodbye and how this can help deal with sadness and feelings when a friendship ends.

Homework

Give out Handout 5 and ask the group members to work through the sheet.

Handout 1 What are friends?

Qualities to value in a friend:

Qualities I can offer a friend:

Characteristics I dislike in friends:

Benefits I get from having friends:

Who I can have as friends:

Handout 2 Starting friendships

Different ways to meet and make friends include:

- Offering to help someone do something;
- Joining a club/society/education class;
- Offering to show someone new around;
- Starting a conversation with someone you do not normally speak to;
- Getting someone you know to introduce you to someone else you would like to meet;
- Starting to talk to someone who has a similar interest to you. This could be theatre, books, music, football and so on;
- Asking someone to join you for a cup of tea or coffee;
- Asking someone if they would like to go with you to an activity or an outing;
- Offering to give someone a lift.

Handout 3 Sustaining friendships

Reasons friendships may change include:

✫ Interests of one or both people changing;
✫ Either person getting a new job;
✫ Either person moving house;
✫ Either person getting married or divorced;
✫ Not spending time together;
✫ Disagreeing with a friend and not making up;
✫ The friend needing help and not getting it;
✫ Being disloyal and feeling guilty;
✫ Not having time to keep the relationship going.

Ways to keep a relationship going may include:

✫ Investing time in it;
✫ Taking an interest in the person;
✫ Giving support;
✫ Keeping in contact;
✫ Agreeing to disagree;
✫ Being honest;
✫ Apologising for something that has offended;
✫ Keeping a shared interest.

Handout 4 When friendships end

Why friendships have ended:

Good ways to end a friendship:

Handout 5 Homework

Qualities I want a friend to have are:

Qualities I can bring to a friendship are:

Characteristics I have that should be avoided are:

Qualities I could develop that would help friendships are:

I could keep a friendship I have by:

I could make a new friend by:

9 Establishing and keeping close relationships

Aim
To explore the nature of close relationships.

Learning Objectives
By the end of the session group members will understand:
- Why people have close relationships;
- How to establish a close relationship;
- What they want from particular relationships;
- How they can manage changes that occur;
- How to cope when a close relationship ends.

Introduction

Whilst encouraging individuals to look at how close relationships can develop, change and end, this session does not require the group facilitator to take on the role of a relationship counsellor. If anyone requires help for particular problems, a referral should be made to an appropriate professional for either medical or counselling support.

The session is designed to raise the group members' awareness of how close relationships function and to explore what will be expected from individuals when they form them. As a group facilitator you need to give thought to the fact that group members may be in:

- Same-sex relationships;
- Good relationships;
- Bad relationships;
- The process of ending a relationship or have recently ended a relationship.

It therefore is reasonable to assume there are likely to be sensitive issues that will be touched on during the session. Clear boundaries need to be established at the beginning of the session, reminding people:

- About confidentiality within the group;
- That personal attacks or criticism must not happen;
- That respect must be shown to all types of diversity in relationships;
- That sensitivity is to be shown;
- That it is the right of each person not to discuss any issues they feel sensitive about.

Care needs to be taken during the session that it is not dominated by any one person's difficulties. Agree with the group that, if a sensitive issue is touched upon, time can be taken out of the group or an impromptu group break arranged to get things back to normal. As long as the above arrangements are in place and you are prepared, the group should run without any difficulties.

Preparing to do the activities

Why have close relationships?

Use the example reasons for having close relationships and what the benefits are, or think about some of your own. Also think about some disadvantages. Examples from experience are always useful to bring a reason to life and give it meaning. When doing the activity it may be necessary to ask group members to expand or explain some of the reasons they put forward.

Making it happen

Again, examples of how close relationships can happen are useful. You will probably be able to use your own experience of how some of your own relationships developed to add to the material supplied and the ideas put forward by group members. Relationships tend to develop at their own pace and in their own way, but looking back on how something happened can give you good insight into what made it happen and work for you.

What I want

This is a good exercise to do yourself before the session. Think through the implications and what you might do to address them. How do you feel when doing the exercise? Does it bring up any feelings or make you realise something you did not think about before? How might similar feelings affect someone in the group?

Managing changes

Think about the changes that have occurred in some of your own relationships. What were they and how did they affect the relationship? Did some of them have a small effect and others a huge impact? What, for you, made the change something you felt strongly about? Did the other person do something that went against a value that you felt was important? Was it a betrayal of trust? Did the changes and how you felt about them emphasise what is important for you in a relationship? As these issues are highlighted for group members, they can be linked back to the importance of the person knowing what is important for them in a relationship and knowing what is important for the other person involved.

Moving on

This activity is likely to bring out emotional difficulties and there is a chance that someone in the group may be in the process of ending a relationship. It is therefore very important that the activity brings out that endings to relationships occur in many contexts. People grow apart, one partner may have been unfaithful, deceptions may have occurred, there may have been financial problems, a close friend may have different interests, moved to another job, what each person wants from the relationship may have changed and so on. It needs to be emphasised that moving on is a part of life and that difficulties – painful as they sometimes are – can be worked through.

Explain that it is normal to feel angry or hurt and that this is part of the grieving process when a relationship ends.

The parts of the activity that should be emphasised are the ways to deal with feelings and the opportunities that can be presented when a relationship ends. There may be one or two people in the group who can give examples of how they have gone on to do other things and made changes that they have found very satisfying and are glad about. Again, thinking about endings you have experienced yourself and what worked well will help to prepare you to lead the activity.

It is important that you plan so that the activity ends on a positive note and individuals have reason to feel positive about any difficulties they may be experiencing.

9 Establishing close relationships

Objectives	Activity	Time (in mins)
To remind the group members about what was learnt in the previous session, to give an opportunity to discuss issues or feedback about homework and to set aims for the current session	**Review previous session, obtain feedback from homework and set aims for this session**	10
To explore the benefits and disadvantages of close relationships	**Why have close relationships?**	20
To look at ways in which a close relationship can develop	**Making it happen**	15
To examine individual perceptions of a particular relationship	**What I want**	15
BREAK		10
To investigate changes that can occur and how they can be managed	**Managing changes**	25
To explore methods of coping with the ending of relationships	**Moving on**	20
To check outcomes have been achieved and to explain the homework assignment	**Review the session and set homework assignment**	5

9 Activity guidelines

Review the previous session, obtain feedback from the homework and state the aims of the current session

Ask group members, in turn, to state something they learnt in the previous session. Discuss any points raised concerning the homework and outline the aims for the current session.

Why have close relationships?

Distribute Handout 1. Point out to the group that people form a wide variety of close relationships. These may include being best friends, family, marriage and both opposite and same-sex partners. (Be aware that some individuals may be in same-sex relationships.) Give people a couple of minutes to think and write down a few reasons for forming close relationships on Handout 1. Now ask individuals to suggest their own reasons and write these on a flip-chart. Examples are:

- For support;
- To avoid being lonely;
- To have sex;
- To have someone to talk to;
- To belong;
- For security;
- Because everybody does;
- To have a family;
- To protect someone;
- For friendship;
- To have company;
- For money;
- To get respect;
- To be looked after;
- For companionship;
- To have someone to do things for;
- For intellectual conversation;
- To be loved.

The above are the gains people get from a relationship. Next, give people a couple of minutes to think about and write down on Handout 1 what they think might be the disadvantages of having close relationships and then have individuals call them out. Examples might be:

- Need to make time for the other person;
- Have to listen to their problems;
- Have to make compromises;
- Sometimes do things they want and I do not;
- Be faithful;
- Be honest with the other person.

Making it happen

For this exercise, ask the group members to discuss different ways in which a relationship can develop into a close one. Write the conclusions on a flip-chart and discuss them. Some suggestions are given in Handout 2, which can be handed out at the end of the activity.

What I want

Give out Handout 3, ask the group members to think about a relationship they have with someone and ask them to write down what they want from that relationship and what they think the other person may want from it. When they have done this, ask if what they want corresponds with what the other person wants or not. Some probably will not know what the other person wants or not be sure about it. The other person may want different things. That may work or it may prevent the relationship becoming closer. Discuss ideas about how these aspects of a relationship can be resolved.

Managing changes

Divide everyone into two groups. Ask Group 1 to compile a list of changes that can happen and things that can go wrong during a relationship. Ask Group 2 to think of a list of strategies to manage changes and difficulties that may arise. Suggestions are provided in Handout 4, which can be handed out at the end of the activity.

When the lists are complete, bring the groups back together and have Group 1 feed back first. Allow Group 2 members to add to the list presented by Group 1. Then ask those in Group 2 to present their list of strategies, with Group 1 adding any ideas of their own.

Moving on

Ask group members to say what it feels like when a close relationship comes to an end. Write the key words up on a flip-chart or white-board.

When a comprehensive list has been completed, explain that these feelings are normal and natural, and discuss with the group ways to deal with them. Get the group to think of ideas.

Lastly, lead the group in a discussion of what opportunities are presented when a relationship ends. Again, list possible opportunities on a flip-chart.

Suggestions for the above are shown in Handout 5 which can be handed out at the end of the activity.

Homework

Give out Handout 6 and ask the group members to decide on a friendship they want to improve. Once that has been decided, they then complete the handout and start putting the actions they have decided on into practice.

Handout 1 Why have close relationships?

Why have close relationships?	Disadvantages of close relationships

Handout 2 Making it happen

Ways in which a relationship can develop into a close one include:

- Spending time together to get to know each other;
- Building trust or confidence in each other;
- Listening to each other;
- Doing things together;
- Sharing values;
- Discussing problems;
- Sharing private thoughts;
- Reaching an understanding about what each wants from the relationship;
- Sharing feelings/emotions/anxieties/successes;
- Congratulating each other.

Handout 3 What I want

What I want from my relationship with _____ is:	What I think _____ wants is:

Session 9: Establishing and keeping close relationships

Handout 4 Managing changes

Changes that can happen and things that can go wrong in relationships include:

★ Disagreeing over children;
★ Wanting different things;
★ One person becoming ill;
★ Jealousy;
★ Dishonesty;
★ Spending too much time apart;
★ Debt/gambling/drinking too much;
★ Not discussing problems;
★ Attitudes or values changing.

Strategies to manage changes and difficulties may include:

★ Talking to other people about problems;
★ Getting other perspectives or opinions;
★ Not making decisions in the heat of the moment;
★ Involving professional help such as debt counsellors, Relate, family planning etc;
★ Acknowledging that relationships will not always be perfect;
★ Making time to talk about problems or anxieties;
★ Acknowledging that things can change in relationships;
★ Agreeing that problems can be worked through.

Handout 5 Moving on

When a relationship ends you might feel:

- Angry
- Rejected
- Relief
- Lonely
- Guilty
- Depressed
- Sad
- A loss of confidence
- Confused
- That you do not want to get hurt again.

Ways to deal with these feelings include:

- Talking to someone about how you feel;
- Writing about it (a letter that is never posted);
- Doing something to keep occupied;
- Seeking professional help if you are depressed;
- Planning treats to look forward to, such as a meal with another friend or doing something you enjoy.

Opportunities that present themselves when a relationship ends can include:

- A chance to learn from mistakes;
- Rethinking what is wanted from a new relationship;
- A chance to do things you would not have done had the relationship continued;
- More time to spend with other people;
- A chance to take up new interests.

Handout 6 Improving a relationship

What I want from my relationship with _____ is:
_____
_____
_____
_____

What I do not want is:
_____
_____
_____
_____
_____
_____

What _____ wants from our relationship is:
_____
_____
_____
_____

What he/she does not want is:
_____
_____
_____
_____
_____
_____

I can improve my friendship/relationship by:

1
_____
_____

2
_____
_____

3
_____
_____

10 Appreciating other points of view

Aim

To develop a greater appreciation of other people's feelings and views, and how this affects interactions and relationships.

Learning Objectives

By the end of the session group members will understand:

☆ What is to be gained by understanding other viewpoints;

☆ What stops people seeing other viewpoints;

☆ Strategies that help to understand other viewpoints;

☆ What effect seeing other viewpoints has on interacting with other people and developing relationships with them.

Introduction

This session explains the importance of being able to see, understand and appreciate the views of other people. It encourages people to develop their awareness that others have emotions, anxieties, expectations and ways of seeing things that might differ from their own. Being able to appreciate these viewpoints and respond in an appropriate way is an important element in successful interactions with others and developing good relationships. The skills learnt from Session 7 (Learning to Listen) are clearly linked and support what is provided here.

Many people may be isolated, live in supported or residential accommodation and be unaware of how their lack of ability to see other viewpoints can affect their ability to interact with others.

The session encourages the notion that there may be a number of solutions to many interaction problems when they are explored from different viewpoints. It will also enable people to:

☆ Resolve conflicts;
☆ Avoid hurting other people;
☆ Share experiences or feelings with others;
☆ Understand the impact their actions can have on others;
☆ Feel less isolated;
☆ Understand how other people might see them.

It is easy to lose sight of other viewpoints when we are under pressure, stressed or have other serious matters on our mind. This also holds true when we are isolated or if a person has not been encouraged to value others. Some of these thoughts will strike a chord with most group facilitators when looking back on their own experiences.

Preparing to do the activities

Why bother!

Some people can find it difficult to see things from other viewpoints. Time spent on exploring what this actually means is time well spent. You will also need to think through what some group members mean by their suggestions. When possible, get the person who made a suggestion to expand and explain it. Giving examples helps individuals to understand better. Go though the list provided and think up examples from your own experience, or make some up.

Experiencing is believing

Again, it is helpful to have an example situation to demonstrate what is needed for the exercise. It is better if the group members are able to use situations from their own experience. This makes it easier to relate the learning to real-life situations. Do remember, though, that some group members may be reluctant to discuss what they consider personal in an open group. Do not force the issue and use the examples given in Handout 1 as required.

Learning to see

You should be able to add to the list of things that stop people from seeing other viewpoints by looking back on times when you have been unable, or unwilling, to see other viewpoints. Acknowledging that sometimes you have not seen another viewpoint because you were stressed, too proud, or did not want to lose face, can give people permission to be open and honest in this exercise. It acknowledges that everyone gets it wrong from time to time.

Negotiating a compromise

People often see making a compromise as allowing someone else get the better of them, and see negotiating as an opportunity for them to get the better of someone else. Examine the meaning outlined in the exercise and your own feelings about these issues. Discussion can bring out ideas similar to those listed, which must be corrected.

Again, it is very helpful if you think back to when you went through the process of negotiating a compromise. As well as going through the steps outlined in this exercise, recall your emotions when you were going through each stage. Discussing how it feels with the group can be very useful. Many feelings may be present on different occasions, depending on the situation, including:

- Embarrassment
- Anxiety
- A sense of fun
- Satisfaction that it has been successful
- A feeling of being included and considered.

Some of these feelings may come up in the 'Learning to see' activity when considering what stops people seeing other viewpoints, and they can be seen as negative. Explain that these normal emotions are more than compensated for by the positive feelings experienced.

10 Appreciating other points of view

Objectives	Activity	Time (in mins)
To remind group members about what was learnt in the previous session, to give an opportunity to discuss issues or feedback about homework and to set aims for the current session	Review previous session, obtain feedback from homework and set aims for this session	10
To gain an understanding of why it is essential to know what other people think	Why bother?	15
To examine a situation to see how knowing different viewpoints can help us to reach better outcomes	Experiencing is believing	30
BREAK		10
To explore what stops people seeing other viewpoints	Learning to see	25
To look at ways of negotiating a compromise	Negotiating a compromise	25
To check outcomes have been achieved and to explain the homework assignment	Review the session and set homework assignment	5

10 Activity guidelines

Review the previous session, obtain feedback from homework and state the aims of the current session

Ask group members what they felt was the most important thing they learnt in the last session. Discuss any points raised concerning the homework and outline the aim for this session.

Why bother!

Briefly discuss what seeing things from someone else's viewpoint means and then ask group members to state what they think are the advantages of being able to see something from another viewpoint. Suggestions are provided in Handout 1.

Positive Interaction Skills

Once this has been explored adequately, ask what disadvantages anyone can see. Again, some suggestions are given in Handout 1.

Discuss the disadvantages briefly and how they stand up against what is to be gained. End the activity by giving out Handout 1.

Experiencing is believing

Divide the group into three subgroups and ask group members to come up with a situation from their own experience. Ask them: if they had seen the situation from the other person's viewpoint would it have helped them to reach a better outcome or avoided a difficult situation? If group members find this difficult to do, distribute Handout 2 and assign one situation to each subgroup. Ask them to explore how the people in the situations would benefit from being able to see the problem from another viewpoint. When they have completed this, ask each subgroup to present their situation to everyone and to explain how seeing it from another viewpoint would have helped in each case.

Learning to see

Form three new subgroups and get each one to think of ideas about what stops people from seeing things from other viewpoints. These can be written on a large sheet of paper. When completed, ask each subgroup to share their ideas with the whole group. Some suggestions are provide in Handout 3.

Discuss the suggestions briefly, add any others that you feel are important and distribute Handout 3.

Negotiating a compromise

Have a discussion with the group about the meaning of 'negotiating a compromise'. Ensure that they understand that it means 'coming up with a solution that all parties involved are happy with'. Explain that it is not about:

- Getting the upper hand;
- Getting one over on someone else;
- Dominating or forcing the other person to agree;
- Allowing someone else to be dominant;
- Being humiliated;
- Being bullied.

When the above is clear, ask each subgroup to think of ideas about the steps they should go through when reaching a compromise with someone. Suggestions should include the ideas listed in Handout 4. When the ideas have been exhausted distribute Handout 4 to be kept as a reference.

Homework

Give out Handout 5 and ask the group members to choose a situation in which they are currently involved where it would be helpful to be aware of another person's viewpoint and go through the process.

Handout 1 Why bother?

Advantages of being able to see things from someone else's viewpoint include:

- It helps to avoid upsetting someone else;
- It provides insight so that a decision can be made to back down;
- It helps with reaching compromises;
- It enables us to agree boundaries;
- It makes it easier to get on with other people;
- It helps with making requests reasonable and appropriate;
- It can avoid falling out with other people;
- It helps when looking at ways to achieve what both people want;
- It enables sensitivity to other people's needs.

Disadvantages include:

- Not always getting your own way;
- The danger of being thought a wimp;
- Sometimes having to put other people first.

Handout 2 Other viewpoint situations

Situation 1

John and Jill have been married for two years. She is 19 and he is 20. They have a one-year-old son, Jason. John works hard and often does overtime to provide extra luxuries for the home. He sees his role as providing everything for the family and feels that he should be able to relax doing his hobbies and go out with his mates when not working or doing up the house. Jill looks after Jason, does all the cleaning and washing and gets up at night to see to Jason when necessary. She seldom gets a break from looking after Jason, feels isolated, cut off from all her old friends and feels she is missing out not having a career. John now wants them to have another child.

Situation 2

Mary has worked as a shop assistant for two years. She feels she is good at her job and has often acted as supervisor when the supervisor has been off sick. The supervisor has left the company and a new supervisor, Janet, has been appointed. Mary thinks Janet is very nice, but resents being told what to do by her, as Mary thought she would be given the job. Mary refuses to carry out an instruction given to her by Janet and storms into the manager's office to complain about her.

Situation 3

Peter works for the same company as Jane and has fancied her for a long time but said nothing. He thinks she is a real stunner. When they meet in the corridor or restaurant she always has a bright smile and says 'Good-morning' or 'Hello'. One day he comes across her by the photocopying machine. She seems very upset about something and is in tears. He thinks this is his chance to take advantage, be sympathetic and then ask her out.

Handout 3 Learning to see

Things that get in the way of being able to see other viewpoints include:

- Not listening;
- Shouting the other person down;
- Not being willing to compromise;
- Thinking that self-interest is always most important;
- Not knowing what is important to the other person;
- Being selfish;
- Not asking the other person what their anxieties are;
- Talking over everyone else;
- A lack of sympathy for other people's feelings.

Handout 4 Negotiating a compromise

Negotiating a compromise means coming up with a solution that all parties are happy with.

It is not about:

- Getting the upper hand;
- Getting one over on someone else;
- Dominating or forcing the other person to agree;
- Allowing someone else to be dominant;
- Being humiliated;
- Being bullied.

When negotiating a compromise you should (including your own):

- Listen to other viewpoints;
- Make sure all viewpoints are understood;
- Ensure clarity about what is least and most important to all parties;
- Consider anxieties and worries people have;
- Find out what each party would be willing to give up;
- Get suggestions from all sides on different ways to achieve outcomes that everyone would be happy with;
- Discuss and agree proposed actions;
- Ensure all parties are happy with the outcome.

Handout 5 Looking at other points of view

Describe the situation:

How I see it:

How _____ sees it

What is important to me:	What is important to _____:
What is least important to me:	What is least important to _____:
My worries/anxieties are:	_____'s worries or anxieties are:
What I would be willing to give up:	What _____ would be willing to give up:

Suggestions to help us find a solution that both of us are happy with are:

Agreed actions:

11 Creating trust and learning to self-disclose

Aim

To investigate the role of 'trust' and 'disclosure' on interactions when forming and sustaining relationships.

Learning Objectives

By the end of the session group members will understand:

- What 'trust' means;
- How to agree 'trust' rules;
- About different levels of trust with different people;
- The benefits of trust and self-disclosure in relationships;
- The different ways disclosures are made;
- The risks involved in disclosure;
- What it is appropriate to disclose in different situations;
- How it feels to make disclosures.

11 Introduction

Trust is at the heart of all relationships. It enables them to develop, continue and end in a satisfactory way. Long term, close and intimate relationships depend on it. An inability to trust can lead to problems developing and can break up what may be a perfectly good relationship.

Individuals need to be able to:

- Trust themselves;
- Be confident in their own ability to be trustworthy to other people;
- Trust their own judgement;
- Have faith in themselves to work for the best in a relationship;
- Be confident in their ability to develop and grow;
- Trust other people in the same way.

How much trust is shared will influence people's perceptions of each other and how close relationships become. A level of trust acceptable to both people in a relationship has to be established before it can develop.

When trust is broken, individuals can choose to work through the issues and repair the damage. Alternatively, both or one party may decide the damage cannot be repaired and end the relationship or make it less close.

The degree of trust also allows people to disclose things about themselves. What is disclosed shows one person to another as they truly are and influences how the other person will respond to them. It will also help the other person to reveal themself. If what one person honestly thinks and feels is revealed, it reduces the chances of misunderstandings and helps to avoid difficulties.

Talking about ourselves – sharing what we feel, think and do – helps to give us deeper insights into the sort of people we are. It helps to break down the separateness that is felt from others and enables intimacy to develop.

Preparing to do the activities

What is trust?

People show trust in each other by disclosing some information about themselves. If that is accepted and reciprocated then another risk can be taken to disclose something else. And so trust builds. If, however, the other person rejects the initial disclosure then the relationship is unlikely to move on to further disclosures or to deepen and may well end. If both feel safe, they will continue building trust until they reach the limit at which they feel completely safe. People may feel secure in some areas of disclosure, but not in others. This activity should emphasise the meaning of trust, how it helps build relationships and the consequences of not taking some risks and beginning to build trust.

As with other activities, looking at what trust means to you and how it has built up in some of your relationships will give you good insight.

Agreeing boundaries

Boundaries need to be realistic. There is no point in setting boundaries that cannot be kept. Ideas about boundaries may change during a relationship, as do values. Trust may grow or diminish depending on events and experiences. These need to be discussed and viewpoints aired as relationships continue.

It should be mentioned that a small amount of mistrust about how much one's self can be trusted, as well as mistrust about others, is healthy. Feeling unsure about one's own ability to cope without the relationship can lead either to being too trusting or being overly suspicious. There may also be areas of mistrust and other areas of great reliability.

Remember that people are not perfect and that we need to be willing to listen, to give honest explanations and be willing to work through and forgive honest mistakes.

How much trust?

This activity needs to highlight judgements about appropriate disclosures in different situations. You might confide to a best friend or your mother about your marital problems, but would it be appropriate to do so to your boss? Are there any circumstances in which this might be appropriate? Would you disclose in the same sort of detail? You might disclose to your boss that you have made a mistake, but would you tell your next customer about it?

Having a look at some of your own relationships and what you feel is appropriate in what circumstances will give you some feeling for the issues. Do remember that you, too, will probably have areas that are sensitive and may divert from being reasonable to other people.

Disclosure fears and gains

To a certain degree, everyone leads a secret life. They may tell deliberate lies, partial lies or omit something, keeping it from the other party. They may do this for a variety of reasons, but fear of the consequences of truthful disclosures or hiding their real selves will feature high on the list. The risks are often more imagined than real.

Think about disclosures you have made fearing imagined consequences. What was the result? Do keep in mind that some people will have fears about people liking them or may have anxieties about how they will handle a relationship if it is allowed to develop. Others may have strong feelings about not being worthy, or have feelings of shame. These may concern thoughts about:

- Self-hate
- Violence
- Suicide
- Same-sex relationships
- Opposite sex

Some people may have fears concerning positive thoughts about themselves, fearing that these will be thought of as boasting. Suggest that a way of dealing with this is to reveal one or two negative disclosures, rather than making them all positive.

How self-disclosure happens

This work links closely to the session on body language. A lot of the same issues emerge. How you dress when meeting someone will disclose something about what you think and feel about them. It also speaks volumes about how you wish other people to see you.

Genuineness and sincerity are very important and are most easily conveyed through being consistent in the message verbally, through body language, touch and action. This also avoids confusion about the message being conveyed.

Listening is another important skill when making disclosures and building trust. When one person makes a disclosure, the other must be willing to listen. That other person, in turn, must be willing to listen when disclosures are made to them. This willingness to listen will help to prevent and manage problems as they arise.

Making disclosures

Starting disclosure sentences beginning with 'I' encourages each person to take responsibility for speaking for themselves. There is a temptation when interacting to begin sentences with 'You': 'You don't like me' or 'You have not considered what I think'. This focuses on the other person and makes a judgement. Much better to own and take responsibility for the message: 'I feel that you don't like me' or 'I don't feel that you have considered what I think.'

This provides a number of advantages:

- It acknowledges what you think or feel, without judging the other person, or accusing them and gives an opportunity for them to reassure or show otherwise in response.
- It is less likely to aggravate the other person.
- Positive statements, like 'I enjoyed that' sound as if you mean them.

Some people may find this exercise difficult as it requires them to disclose their feelings. It can be quite scary as some may not like their own feelings. Emphasise that it is an opportunity to practise disclosures in a safe environment and that group members can choose what feelings they disclose. It may be something simple, like 'I am feeling very uncomfortable with this exercise.' If you feel it appropriate, change the exercise, asking group members to disclose one negative and one positive feeling.

Women may find it more difficult to express feelings about ambition or assertiveness. Men sometimes have difficulty expressing feelings of vulnerability or those that expose sensitivity. Other difficult areas for most can include accepting or paying compliments and feelings of being worthless.

11 Creating trust and learning to self-disclose

Objectives	Activity	Time (in mins)
To remind group members about what was learnt in the previous session, to give opportunity to discuss issues or feedback about homework and set the aims for the current session	Review previous session, obtain feedback from homework and set aim for this session	10
To share a common understanding of what trusting someone means	What is trust?	15
To look at how rules about trust can be agreed by individuals	Agreeing rules	20
To explore how much it is appropriate to trust different people	How much do I trust someone?	15
BREAK		10
To assess fears and gains when making disclosures	Disclosure fears and gains	15
To raise awareness of the different ways disclosure occurs	How disclosure happens	15
To experience how it feels to make disclosures	Making disclosures	15
To check outcomes have been achieved and to explain the homework assignment	Review the session and set homework assignment	5

11 Activity guidelines

Review the previous session, obtain feedback from the homework and state the aims of the current session

Ask each group member to state something from the last session that they have been able to put into practice. Discuss any points raised about the homework and outline the aims for this session.

Session 11: Creating trust and learning to self-disclose 157

What is trust?

Have a discussion with the group members and ask them to define what 'trust' means. Write the conclusions on a flip-chart or white-board. Explain that trust is essential to enable bonding to happen – particularly in close and long-term relationships. When this is understood, pose the question: 'What happens when people do not trust each other?'

Answers may include:

> ★ They can become jealous;
> ★ The relationship breaks up;
> ★ They don't tell each other things;
> ★ It can lead to break-up;
> ★ They don't want to spend time together;
> ★ They become suspicious;
> ★ The relationship is weakened.

Agreeing boundaries

Explain to the group members that when they trust someone they need to understand the boundaries of that trust – otherwise how do we know when we might be breaking it? Setting and agreeing boundaries and making them work entails:

> ★ Taking risks;
> ★ Being willing to listen to explanations or to give honest explanations if boundaries are infringed;
> ★ Being willing to work through misunderstandings and other problems;
> ★ Being willing to forgive honest mistakes.

When the above has been understood, give out Handout 1 and get the group to agree what boundaries or rules it will be helpful for the couple described in Handout 1 to have discussed and agreed before getting married.

How much trust?

Explain to the group that it is not appropriate to show the same level of trust to everyone. It may not be appropriate to trust a work acquaintance with the same information that they might disclose to a personal friend. Getting this right can be tricky. Give out Handout 2 and ask the group members to discuss and answer the questions about what boundaries they set with some of the people listed.

Disclosure fears and gains

Write the headings 'Fears' and 'Gains' on the white-board or a flip-chart. Ask the group members to state their fears first, which are likely to include:

- Being rejected;
- Being misunderstood;
- Saying too much;
- Having what you say used against you;
- Confidentiality not being respected;
- Being humiliated;
- Having to choose between friends.

When completed, move on to list what gains they see from making disclosures. These may include:

- A closer relationship;
- Being understood;
- Being liked;
- Feeling included;
- Avoiding loneliness;
- Feeling worthwhile;
- Better self-esteem;
- Having someone to talk to about problems;
- Feeling less isolated.

End by pointing out that the benefits make the risks worthwhile.

How self-disclosure happens

Give out Handout 3, read through it and discuss the statements made.

Making disclosures

Divide the group members into pairs. Say they have about five minutes in which to make three disclosures to each other that the other person does not know. The disclosures should be about feelings, positive and negative, and start 'I ...' Examples are:

> * I feel lonely sometimes;
> * I get embarrassed when my husband starts boasting;
> * My job as a nurse make me feel really worthwhile – that what I do matters;
> * I'm really proud of myself for doing this.

Finish the activity by having everyone discuss how it felt to make the disclosures and asking them how body language, the words used, the way in which things were said, and so on, affected how the disclosures were heard and believed.

Homework

Give out Handout 4 and ask the group members to rate themselves for building trust and making disclosures and identify the areas they will work on to make improvements.

Handout 1 Boundaries situation

Situation 1

John and Ann are planning to get married. He is very good looking, fit and fanatical about football. He is a junior manager in a cosmetics company and has a reputation for having sexual relationships with a number of the women who are employed by the company. He likes to flirt and sees himself as a man's man, with little time for domestic issues – those, in his mind, are for women to sort out. He would like children, but imagines that Ann will look after them and does not see children altering his way of life. The company is not doing very well and all the managers have had to take a cut in salary.

The couple have contracted to buy a large detached, slightly run-down house in a good area. The mortgage will stretch their finances to the limit and John will have to do overtime to enable them to keep up payments.

Ann is very style- and image-conscious, loves shopping and extravagant holidays. She spends money as if is on endless supply and is in debt. She likes to have the latest gadgets and clothes. She is excited about the house John and she are buying and has lots of expensive ideas about how she wants it refurbished. Ann is very possessive and given to jealousy. Her suspicions are aroused when John is even a few minutes late home or he has to work late. Ann enjoys working as a personal assistant to the director of a large insurance company. She would like to have children, but does not want to give up work. She also thinks that John should be just as involved in looking after any children as she is.

What boundaries would it be helpful for John and Ann to discuss and agree before getting married?

Handout 2 Different levels of trust

Consider and compare your perceptions of appropriate boundaries of trust with the people listed below, with other members of the group. Consider the following questions:

- Do different group members have different ideas about appropriate boundaries?
- Are your ideas of boundaries the same as those of the people listed?
- Does not being aware of these boundaries lead to any misunderstanding or problems?
- Do the boundaries keep people at an appropriate closeness to, or at a distance from, you?

A work pal	Your mother/father
A well-known neighbour	A brother/sister
Your grandmother/grandfather	A close friend
Someone you meet at a class	Someone you play a sport with
Your partner/wife/husband	Your manager at work
Someone you supervise	Your son/daughter
Your doctor	A customer/client you know
Your financial adviser/ bank manager	Your uncle/aunt

Handout 3 How self-disclosure happens

Self-disclosure happens:

- **Verbally** – what is said and how it is said. This includes the words used, the tone of voice, pitch, sarcasm and so on.
- **By use of body language** – eye contact, gestures, posture, facial expression, distance apart.
- **Through touch** – a hug, a kiss on the cheek, holding hands, touching someone gently on the shoulder and so on.
- **By actions** – doing what you say you will do, sending letters when away to show you care, giving flowers to show appreciation. Actions disclose more than words.

Note: it is only when you give messages consistently in the above ways that you come across as sincere and genuine. If you do not send consistent messages – verbally and through body language and actions – the other person will find it difficult to interpret your message accurately and trust you.

Handout 4 Trust and disclosure checklist

Rate your skills in the following areas for building trust and making disclosures:

Rate your abilities in the following areas:	Poor				Good
Making disclosures	1	2	3	4	5
Agreeing boundaries	1	2	3	4	5
Appropriateness of disclosures	1	2	3	4	5
Asking for explanations	1	2	3	4	5
Commitment	1	2	3	4	5
Ability to work through problems	1	2	3	4	5
Giving others the benefit of the doubt	1	2	3	4	5
Being forgiving	1	2	3	4	5
Being trustworthy	1	2	3	4	5

The areas I can improve are:

I will do this by:

12 Resolving conflict in relationships

Aim

To investigate the causes of conflicts and a suggested framework for resolving them.

Learning Objectives

By the end of the session group members will understand:

☆ The major sources of conflict;

☆ A framework for resolving them;

☆ Blocks to solutions;

☆ Positive ways to respond.

Introduction

Possibilities for conflict exist everywhere and are inevitable in all ongoing relationships. They may arise out of a difference of opinion, desires, values, interests, misunderstandings, values, interests, competitiveness, family interests or cultural background. In addition, many people lack skills in managing conflicts and have difficulty handling the emotions and stress generated by them.

When people do not know how to manage conflict, the feelings generated can become destructive to the relationship. Resentful feelings may escalate the conflict further and trigger more hostile encounters and can, in the worst cases, result in violence.

When conflict management skills are used, potential conflicts can be averted or defused and turned into a positive source for improved interpersonal relationships. Gains can include:

☆ Personal growth;
☆ Increase in self-esteem;
☆ Building of trust;
☆ An increase of openness and honesty;
☆ Greater confidence in ability to create solutions and succeed.

12 Preparing to do the activities

What's it all about

Think back to some of the relationship conflicts that you have observed and experienced over the years. What were their root causes? Was the thing you were arguing about the problem or was there something more fundamental behind it? Thinking of the root cause and analysing how conflict developed, perhaps showing itself by irritation about small, unimportant things, will help you with examples when working through this exercise with group members.

Resolving conflicts

In order to resolve conflicts, people need to believe that the situation can be worked through. They also need to be careful that they are not putting all their energy into defending their position.

Acknowledging a problem can be very difficult. It means facing the problem with all the inherent fears of what the consequences of this might mean: not getting our own way; or having to state our true feelings, viewpoints and the reality of the situation. It can bring overwhelming emotions to the surface. Sometimes individuals find this combination too much to face and go on living with the situation as best they can.

It demands effort to put feelings about ourself to one side while trying to remain calm and understand someone else's viewpoint. When going through the process step by step it may be enough, especially if in an intense or emotional relationship, just to acknowledge the conflict, what it is about and to understand each other's viewpoint. A short time for both people to give this some thought before continuing to the next steps can be helpful.

All the steps do not need to be completed at one time. In fact, it may be useful to have more than one break before all the steps have been completed. Often just acknowledging the conflict and understanding the other's viewpoint automatically leads to solutions being produced.

Do emphasise the need to review the situation at an agreed date in the future to ensure that everyone is happy with the outcome.

Using the framework

Group members may well think of different answers to the case study. Answers to problems are not the same for everyone. Two different couples will probably come up with two different solutions that work well for them.

If the group is able to devote extra time to this activity, divide the members into two or three subgroups and see what different solutions are presented.

Responses to conflict

The negative blocks listed in Handout 4 prevent individuals from seeing and acknowledging what the conflict is, or how it can be solved. Group members will recognise some of them and be able to relate them to their own experience. Managing conflict is a learned skill. Past experience may have lead individuals into negative behaviour patterns, which have prevented them from being able to work through the difficulties. This may have, in the past, led them into other, negative, behaviours, such as ignoring the difficulties or trying to manipulate the other person into doing what they want or to act in the way they want. The result being that the conflict increases and the other person feels cheated.

Group members may well think of behaviours that are not listed. Examine these and create positive alternatives.

12 Resolving conflict

Objectives	Activity	Time (in mins)
To remind the group members about what was learnt in the previous session, to give an opportunity to discus issues or feedback about homework and set the aims for the current session	Review previous session, obtain feedback from homework and set aim for this session	10
To raise awareness about the causes of conflicts in relationships	What's it all about?	20
To explore a framework to help resolve conflicts	Resolving conflicts	25
BREAK		10
To practise using the 'resolving conflicts' framework	Using the framework	30
To examine blocks to resolving problems and ways of turning them into positive actions	Responses to conflict	20
To check outcomes have been achieved and to explain the homework assignment	Review the session and set homework assignment	5

12 Activity guidelines

Review the previous session, obtain feedback from the homework and state the aims of the current session

Ask group members to state something they learnt in the last session and have been able to improve on. Discuss any points raised concerning the homework and outline the aim for this session.

What's it all about?

Give out Handout 1, read through it and discuss the contents.

Positive Interaction Skills

Resolving conflicts

Give out Handout 2, go through each step of the framework, explaining and discussing the process.

Using the framework

Give out Handout 3, allow the group members time to read through the contents and then, using the case presented, work through the process step by step, writing the conclusions for each step up on a white-board or flip-chart.

Responses to conflict

Explain that from time to time everyone uses negative responses that block their ability to work through difficulties and inhibit working through the framework. Using Handout 4, call out the negative blocks to achieving solutions, listed one by one, and ask the group to think of positive ways to respond in place of the negative block. Give Handout 4 out for reference and ask the group members which of the blocks they are inclined to use most. Can they give examples of when they have used the block as a response? Emphasise what the new responses need to be.

Homework

Distribute Handout 5 and ask the group members to rate their conflict resolution skills, identify areas to work on and write an action plan of how they will do this.

Handout 1 Causes of conflict

Conflicts can arise out of:

☆ ***Wants and needs that are not being met.*** This could be lack of independence, lack of security, a dream or ambition that is important. It might be sexual, wanting to be respected, to be listened to or affection not being expressed.

☆ ***Fears.*** This might be about something that could be lost – something important such as a value or a prized possession, pride, dignity, money, a job, a lifestyle, friends or how one sees oneself.

☆ ***Misunderstandings.*** This might be about feelings, what the other person thinks, not perceiving something as it was intended, jumping to conclusions and making assumptions.

☆ ***Lack of trust.*** This can be caused by lack of disclosures about self, possessiveness, lack of self-esteem or confidence in self, lack of commitment to work through problems, avoidance of issues or breaches of confidences.

☆ ***Feeling of being controlled or wanting to control someone.*** Things must be done just how and when you or the other person wants them to be done.

☆ ***A clash of values, beliefs or boundaries.*** Sometimes values can change through experience and this may cause a clash with the other person. One person may be very honest and the other less so.

Other sources of conflict may include:

☆ Levels of self-esteem;
☆ Different lifestyles;
☆ Different interests;
☆ Ability to change or develop;
☆ Different cultural backgrounds;
☆ Sexual expectations;
☆ Different social or economic background;
☆ Different tastes and preferences.

Handout 2 The framework (1 of 2)

Step 1: Acknowledge the conflict

Tensions may be felt through avoidance, silences or arguments about other minor things. If something is important, it needs to be acknowledged and brought out into the open. You need to choose a good time, keep calm and ask the other person to work on the conflict with you. Avoid cornering the other person and agree a suitable time and place for any discussion. Avoid a threatening or aggressive manner, but be assertive. You must also believe that it is possible to work through the conflict.

Step 2: Make efforts to understand each other's viewpoints

When discussing the issue, state your wishes and feelings honestly and assertively. Listen to the response and clarify anything not understood. Ask the other person for their viewpoint, check that you understand what they are saying and admit to any misperceptions you might have about their viewpoint. Explore each other's viewpoints and explain your own. You are not looking for solutions, but trying to understand each other's view. Try to concentrate on the real conflict, not the person or the symptoms. It is important to get to the root of the conflict. You may have been angry with each other over something unimportant, but what was the real issue?

Step 3: State the conflict in a solvable way that leads to action

The way a conflict is stated or defined can provide a block in itself or make the conflict unsolvable. Admit any mistakes or hurtful actions and agree what the conflict is. For example, Harry has committed himself to doing extra work to earn more money to enable the family to go on holiday. Mary is very unhappy about this as she has a part-time job and is finding herself stressed out looking after their three children – one of whom is disabled. She depended on Harry helping her at weekends – he normally looked after the children on Saturdays. She now thinks she will be unable to cope and that they should give up the idea of a holiday. After agreeing that they should try to go on holiday and that they need the extra money, they define their problem as how to help Mary look after the children on Saturdays and avoid her becoming over-stressed.

Handout 2 The framework (2 of 2)

Step 4: Think up as many possible solutions as possible

Use a sheet of paper and write down all the possible solutions that come to mind. Be creative, do not dismiss something that at first sounds silly or outlandish. Often these ideas can lead to real answers. Do not be critical of any ideas at this stage – throw everything into the pot. For example, ideas for Harry and Mary could include getting their grandparents to look after one of more of the children, getting the children involved in a club or sport activity, having them visit one of their pal's houses, contacting other mothers and forming a club for some mothers to look after the children so others can have free time or Harry might take one or two of the children to work with him.

Step 5: Agree the most suitable solution and implement it

Agree a suitable solution or a combination of solutions. For example, Harry's parents may be very happy to have the children every other week. On the other week, one of the children might visit a friend and the other two go to a club activity for the day.

Step 6: Review and make any necessary adjustments

Having implemented the plan, you need to evaluate how it is working on a regular basis and make any adjustments to allow for changes in circumstances. If it is not working, then you may need to go back and see if you can add any other suggestions and choose a different solution.

Handout 3 The framework – case study

Case study

Paul and Angie have lived together for five years – he is 29 and she is 31. She would like to get married and have children. Paul does not want things to change. He says he wants to go on having a good lifestyle, expensive holidays and enjoying himself. He is too young to settle down. Whenever it is mentioned, he keeps saying he needs more time to build up their small business. If they have children he will not have time to support Angie. He does not need the commitment while building up the business. There will be plenty of time to have children later.

Angie wants to have children while she is still relatively young. She has grown tired of their lifestyle and sees their friends as immature and lacking in responsibility. Lots of her former friends have settled down, got married and have young children.

Paul is beginning to see Angie as a spoilsport and a bit of a misery who has lost her sense of fun and ambition for the business. Paul often goes off with his mates without Angie – though she goes along sometimes, but resents it and makes snide remarks. She repeatedly tells Paul that her mother thinks he is selfish, thoughtless, afraid of real responsibility and should grow up. This often results in rows in which they drag out each other's faults.

The atmosphere at home is often tense. Paul appears happy, but is often irritable and impatient and, Angie thinks, secretive. She wonders what he gets up to when he goes out with his mates. She sometimes thinks he is lying about where he goes and what he does. She has accused him of being deceitful and seeing another woman, which he denies. He says she is too controlling and listens to her mother too much. Angie loves Paul, wants to stay with him, but is not happy with the situation and wants to do something about it.

Handout 4 Responses to conflict

Negative blocks	Positive responses
Wanting to 'win' over the other person or persons involved	Look for solutions that work for everyone involved
Blaming someone else for the problem	Look for the cause of the conflict, including your own contribution to it. Own your own perceptions with 'I' statements
Yelling and shouting	Remain calm
Assuming the other person knows what you feel and think	Be open but tactful – they may not have a clue or be completely wrong in their perceptions
Making excuses to avoid facing something because it is difficult	See problems as something to be worked through and managed
Wallowing in self-pity and negative thoughts	Acknowledge that you have strengths and tell yourself that you can manage
Being rigid and unwilling to be the first to change	Be willing to risk taking the lead in making changes and changing
Making negative comments about the other person	Be specific about the behaviour you want changed
Dwelling on past resentments	Focus on the present and the future
Being aggressive or submissive	Be assertive
Telling yourself you have no choice about the issue	Identify as many solutions as possible and choose the most suitable
Choosing not to listen	Use your active listening skills
Poor timing for discussing the conflict	Choose the best time for all concerned
Irrelevant accusations, put downs and diversions	Keep focused
Allowing your emotions and actions to be dominated by someone else's feelings and actions	Be responsible for your emotions and actions

Handout 5 Conflict resolution skills checklist

Rate yourself on your conflict resolution skills:

Rate your abilities in the following areas:	Poor				Good
Acknowledging conflict	1	2	3	4	5
Understanding other viewpoints	1	2	3	4	5
Explaining your own viewpoint	1	2	3	4	5
Defining the conflict and stating it in a solvable way	1	2	3	4	5
Thinking up alternative solutions	1	2	3	4	5
Agreeing a solution	1	2	3	4	5
Implementing and keeping to agreements	1	2	3	4	5
Reviewing and making adjustments to make solutions work	1	2	3	4	5

The areas I can improve are:

I will do this by:

13. Being assertive and handling criticism

Aim

To examine the principles of assertive behaviour and learn how to deal with criticism.

Learning Objectives

By the end of the session group members will understand:

☆ What being assertive means;

☆ How to identify appropriate assertive behaviour;

☆ The benefits of responding in an assertive way;

☆ How to use positive self-talk;

☆ How to deal with criticism.

13. Introduction

All interaction entails the use of assertiveness skills. This includes working with colleagues, friendships, intimate and sexual relationships, building trust, setting boundaries and so on. Everyone may, on different occasions, act aggressively, assertively or non-assertively. For example, a person may choose to act non-assertively because they are not feeling well, or because they feel it is inappropriate to take up the issue at that particular time. They may be stressed and act in an aggressive manner towards someone who makes a simple request.

However, many people lack the skills to be able to share their wants, needs, thoughts and feelings. Some may behave aggressively because it is how they have learnt to get their own way, regardless of the needs of others. Others will behave in a non-assertive or passive way that allows others to take advantage of or bully them. Either of these behaviour reactions can lead to resentment, lack of self-esteem, feelings of worthlessness and anger.

Within relationships, assertiveness skills help people to cope with negative behaviour from others and to behave positively towards others. Actions give an opportunity for the relationship to develop and solutions to be sought where conflict of interests may be involved.

If young people are not taught assertiveness skills, their maladaptive behaviour is likely to stay with them for years and will become very difficult to change. They will also have great difficulty resisting peer pressure.

The advantages of using assertiveness skills in relationships include:

- An increase of awareness in other people about how you feel about their behaviour, giving them an opportunity to change. For example, if Peter has a habit of criticising Mary in front of his mother and she tells him how much it upsets her, he can choose to stop doing it;
- If what one person wants clashes with what another person wants, solutions can be explored;
- Improved self-esteem;
- Good communication being established in relationships and the ability to adapt to change is enhanced;
- Openness, avoiding hidden agendas, resentments and misunderstandings.
- People feeling better after they have raised issues and their view has been acknowledged and taken into account.

Preparing to do the activities

The three types of behaviour

It is important that group members are able to distinguish the different types of behaviour and understand what assertive behaviour is. This will enable them to identify their own maladaptive behaviour, recognise it in others and find positive ways to respond to it. Looking at your own behaviour and examining what happens when you are aggressive, passive or assertive will help you with examples. Incidents that have occurred in the sessions may also be useful to illustrate points with the group. It also gets group members into the habit of looking at their own behaviour, reaching conclusions about it and deciding on action.

Identifying behaviours

This exercise is intended to reinforce the group members' ability to identify the different types of behaviour in others and in themselves and to work out appropriate responses to it.

Feelings

Even feeling good can be difficult to deal with. It may give rise to bursts of energy or feelings of guilt if a partner is having a bad time. It is important that people learn to recognise and take responsibility for these feelings no matter how scary they may be. It can be destructive both for minds and bodies to repress feelings. Feelings of anger, guilt or frustration can lead to anxiety and depression. There is evidence to show that it may also influence some physical diseases.

Feelings not expressed at the time can remain bottled up for years and then, unexpectedly, emerge and be much more difficult to deal with.

When disclosing feelings, it is essential that other people are not blamed for them. Something someone else has said or done may cause someone to be angry, but the other person may be totally unaware of the effect the action has had, or they may even have being trying to please. It is helpful to focus on the behaviour, not the person.

Being positive

This exercise is useful as a strategy to help build up confidence in our ability to carry through the assertive responses. An examination of your own feelings when waiting to ask for a pay-rise or when called on to be assertive in a difficult situation, will give you plenty of negative self-talk and positive self-talk to use as examples.

Dealing with criticism

Criticism, if given to people in a very negative way, can be very difficult to deal with in a positive and assertive manner. Often it may give rise to anger, embarrassment, feelings of being got at, or that it is unjustified. However, the ability to use criticism in a positive way enables people to develop an awareness of themselves and to change their behaviour in light of that knowledge. It can have a radical effect on any relationships that are formed and how they can develop.

The strategy provided in Handout 4 provides steps to enable group members to stand back, take control of an event and work through it in a positive and assertive way, rather than reacting in an aggressive or passive manner with their guaranteed negative outcomes.

Critical moments

Dealing with emotions when criticism is levelled directly at you is dificult. This exercise gives an opportunity to begin dealing with the feelings and the process involved. Dealing with a large number of criticisms can be demoralising for anyone. Do not allow anyone to have more than five criticisms and if anyone seems vulnerable reduce this number. Also, ensure that everyone criticised has at least one positive statement made about them at the end of the session. Ask them how it felt to have something nice said about them after the critical comments.

13 Activity guidelines

Objectives	Activity	Time (in mins)
To remind the group members about what was learnt in the previous session, to give an opportunity to discuss issues or feedback about homework and to set the aims for the current session	**Review the previous session, obtain feedback from homework and set the aim for this session**	10
To reach an understanding about what being assertive means	**The three types of behaviour**	15
To practise identifying different types of behaviour	**Identifying behaviours**	15
To understand the necessity of owning feelings and acting accordingly	**Feelings!**	20
BREAK		10
To explore the use of positive self-talk	**Being positive**	15
To learn how to manage criticism	**Dealing with criticism**	10
To practise dealing with criticism	**Critical moments**	20
To check outcomes have been achieved and to explain the homework assignment	**Review the session and set homework assignment**	5

13 Activity guidelines

Review the previous session, obtain feedback from the homework and state the aims of the current session

Ask the group members what was the most important thing they learnt in the last session. Discuss any points raised concerning the homework and outline the aims for this session.

Three types of behaviour

Go through the different types of behaviour outlined in Handout 1, using the different headings on a flip-chart and asking the group members to contribute their ideas. Ensure that the points listed on the handout are included. When completed, give out copies of the handout.

Identifying behaviours

Distribute Handout 2. Divide the group into subgroups or pairs, or get the members to work individually. Ask them to identify which type of behaviour the situation and response columns represent. When this has been completed, ask the members to think of situations and responses they gave, which were either non-assertive or aggressive, and to think of an assertive response. When completed, these responses can be shared with the larger group as appropriate.

Feelings

Give out Handout 3 and go through the contents with the group members. Complete the activity by asking people to think of times when they have blamed others for how they were feeling, and rephrase these as assertive statements taking responsibility for their own feelings. This work can be competed in pairs or small groups, as appropriate. When sufficient time has been allowed, invite a few people to share their 'blaming' and 'assertive statements' with the whole group.

Being positive

Explain to the group that everyone, in their own mind, talks to themself in both negative and positive ways that either undermine or reinforce confidence. This can seriously affect the ability to be assertive. Using a flip-chart, ask the group members to call out negative self-thoughts they have had when trying to be assertive. Examples might be:

- I'm a failure
- Why bother
- Nobody pays any attention to me
- I'm not important
- He never considers me, so saying something is a waste of time
- She doesn't listen to anything I suggest

When completed, substitute ideas for alternative positive self-talk. Examples might be:

> ★ What I think is important.
> ★ I feel anxious but I have the ability to do this.
> ★ I have the right to say how I feel.
> ★ Keep calm. I can cope.
> ★ There may be a good explanation. She will explain when I tell her how I feel.
> ★ I know she/he can't please everyone, but I need to tell him/her what I feel.

Emphasise to the group members the importance of practising making positive assertions to themselves. It will help them immensely when they want to act in an assertive way.

Dealing with criticism

Give out Handout 4 and go through each of the steps outlined with the group.

Critical moments

Give out some sheets of paper and ask group members to write down five criticisms, both true and untrue, that have been made about them in the past and how they might respond assertively to them. When this has been completed, divide the group into pairs and get them to exchange lists. Now, taking turns and alternating making a criticism and responding to it, one partner makes a criticism and the other responds assertively. When this activity has been completed, ask each pair to make a complimentary statement to each other. For example: 'I like working with you', 'You did that really well', 'You are a good listener. I always enjoy talking to you'.

Homework

Give out Handout 5 and ask everyone to rate their assertiveness skills: identify areas they need to work on and plan how they will do this.

Handout 1 Three types of behaviour *(1 of 3)*

Non-assertive behaviour

This means that you:

- Have difficulty saying what you think, feel, want or believe;
- Do not believe that you have rights;
- Are reluctant to speak up for yourself;
- Think other people have more rights than you;
- Find it difficult to make reasonable requests from other people;
- Avoid taking responsibility for your own feelings and actions;
- Blame other people for your feelings and actions.

The results of being non-assertive are:

- Feelings of resentment and anger;
- Feelings of powerlessness;
- Low self-esteem;
- Being bullied;
- Unequal relationships;
- Not being respected;
- Giving others what they want and ignoring your own needs;
- Avoiding taking risks and making changes;
- Frustration in relationships;
- Indecision;
- Being apologetic.

Typical body language displayed:

- Talking softly;
- Drooping shoulders;
- Limp handshake;
- Poor eye-contact;
- People invading your body space;
- Looking down at the floor.

Handout 1 Three types of behaviour (2 of 3)

Aggressive behaviour

This means that you:

- Do not respect the rights of others;
- Say what you think, feel, want or believe without thought for others;
- Want to win at all costs;
- Attack other people verbally;
- Bully others into doing what you want;
- Use power or position to get your own way.

The results of being aggressive are that you:

- Are feared;
- Are not liked;
- Have unequal relationships;
- Are unfriendly;
- Have low self-esteem;
- Have poor interactions and relationships;
- Are not trusted;
- Are resented;
- Are avoided by others.

Typical body language displayed:

- A loud voice;
- A vice-like handshake;
- Use of threatening, abusive, accusing, often sarcastic language;
- Intruding the body space of others;
- In extreme cases, physical violence;
- Squaring up to others in a threatening manner.

Handout 1 Three types of behaviour (3 of 3)

Assertive behaviour

This is being able to:

- Say what you think, feel, want or believe in ways that do not infringe the rights of others;
- Be open, honest, direct;
- Stand up for your rights, while respecting the rights of others;
- Make reasonable requests from others;
- Confidently and openly communicate your views to others;
- Refuse unreasonable requests from others;
- Find compromises where conflict exists;
- Take responsibility for yourself, your feelings and actions without blaming or judging others.

Benefits from acting in an assertive manner include:

- Feeling good about yourself;
- Good self-esteem;
- Being able to clarify misperceptions;
- Developing good equal relationships;
- Building trust with others;
- Being able to be more open;
- Gaining a greater knowledge of other people;
- Avoiding unnecessary conflicts or aggression;
- Being able to communicate your ideas/feelings without infringing the rights of others;
- Having a clearer idea of boundaries and commitment in any relationships.

Handout 2 Identifying behaviours (1 of 2)

Situation	Response	Behaviour
You go into a shop to buy a jacket. The sales assistant tells you it fits perfectly and looks fine, but you are not sure.	'I don't know, but if you think it's OK I'll have it.'	
Peter is always late for work. His boss asks him if he owns an alarm clock.	'That's got nothing to do with you.'	
You have been given extra responsibility at work and feel that it warrants a pay rise.	'I'd like to talk about my pay in relation to the extra responsibility I've been given. Could we meet next week to discuss it?'	
Your flat mate is playing loud music while you are trying to study.	'Turn that bloody music down!'	
Jane has always worked late when requested to do so. She has bought tickets to go to the theatre as a special birthday treat for her mother. Her boss asks her to work late.	'OK, I'll ring my mother and see if she can go with someone else.'	
A colleague has taken credit from your boss for work that you did.	'Why did you let the boss think you did the work when you know I did it? I want you to tell her the truth.'	

Session 13: Being assertive and handling criticism

Handout 2 Identifying behaviours *(2 of 2)*

Situation	Your response	Assertive response

Handout 3 Feelings *(1 of 2)*

Feelings can be difficult to deal with when being assertive. They give rise to both physical and emotional reactions within you. For example:

Emotion	Reaction
Anxiety:	Sweating
	Palpitations
	Erratic breathing
	Upset stomach
When feeling good:	Relaxed
	Lots of energy
	Enthusiasm
Sadness:	Tearful
	Tiredness
	Lack of energy

Ways to release feelings include:

☆ Thinking things through;
☆ Reflecting on the situation;
☆ Getting the situation into perspective;
☆ Writing down how you feel;
☆ Doing physical activity like sport.

However, the best way to release feelings is to say how we feel. When doing this, it is important that you do not blame other people for how you feel.

Blaming statements	Assertive statements
'You make me feel angry when you ignore what I have asked you.'	'I feel angry when you ignore what I ask.'
'You make me feel jealous and upset me when you talk about your relationship with Paul.'	'I feel jealous and upset when you talk about your relationship with Paul.'

Handout 3 Feelings *(2 of 2)*

Think of some situations when you have blamed someone for your feelings and rephrase them to take responsibility for your feelings.

Blaming statements	Assertive statements

Handout 4 Dealing with criticism

Step 1

Listen carefully. Try not to react. Check your understanding of what is being said by summing up their statement. If you have got it right, ask for an example of the behaviour.

('You say I ignore you when we go out with friends. Can you give me an example of when I did this?') Do not admit it is true, deny it, sulk or walk away. You are trying to understand what has upset the other person.

Step 2

Consider what has been said. It may be all true, partly true or completely untrue. At this stage, you may need time to think through what has been said. The other person may be very angry or you may feel upset or angry and need time to calm down. If time is needed, say you need time to think about it and agree a time to talk about it later.

Step 3

If the accusation is true, say so, state how you feel about it and ask how it has affected the other person. ('Yes, I did lie to my mother. I am sorry I did it. Has it made things very difficult for you?')

If it is partly true, admit the part that is true and deny what is untrue. ('Yes, I did lie to my mother, I'm sorry I did that, but I did not steal money from her purse.')

If the accusation is not true, say so, and ask why the person thought it. ('No, I did not lie to my mother. I told her the truth. What makes you think I lied?')

Step 4

Review what has been said, how you feel, what you have learnt about yourself and decide if you want to make any changes to your behaviour. If your behaviour has upset someone, you may want to ensure that does not happen again. If – as in the example – you had lied, you might decide to tell your mother the truth and avoid lying in the future.

Handout 5 Assertiveness and handling criticism checklist

Rate your skills in the following areas for assertiveness and handling criticism.

Rate your abilities in the following areas:	Poor				Good
Identifying my behaviour type	1	2	3	4	5
Identifying the behaviour type of others	1	2	3	4	5
Owning my own feelings	1	2	3	4	5
Using positive self-talk	1	2	3	4	5
Dealing with criticism	1	2	3	4	5
Being assertive	1	2	3	4	5

The areas I can improve are:

I will do this by:

14 Overcoming shyness and loneliness

Aim

To explore ways of dealing with shyness and loneliness.

Learning Objectives

By the end of the session group members will understand:

☆ The effects of shyness;

☆ How to manage shyness;

☆ The positive and negative effects of loneliness;

☆ Methods to relieve loneliness;

☆ How to break down barriers to overcome loneliness.

Introduction

Shyness

Many people, even though they may appear quietly confident, are affected by worries about what other people think about them. The shyness of some others may be obvious to anyone. It may be the person who blushes and is easily embarrassed. It may also be the loud-mouth who keeps butting in and cannot stop talking. It may be the person who is always joking and uses this as a cover.

Shy people may be referred to as bashful, timid, wary, uneasy in company. Whatever it is called, shyness can play a huge part in stopping a person from making personal contacts and being able to interact in a way which allows relationships to develop.

The techniques outlined here are not magical and will require lots of motivation and practice to put into effect. At times, enthusiasm may wane and at other times, when success has been experienced, it will soar. At times when enthusiasm is low, if people think about what life is like with shyness and how it affects them and then think about what life would be like if they were more able to manage it, it will help to maintain their motivation.

Loneliness

Loneliness is a distressing personal experience. It is different from being alone. One can be alone, but not lonely. A person may also feel lonely within a relationship, or be surrounded by colleagues or relatives and still be lonely. Relationships may have broken down, there may be a lack of satisfactory communication or connection.

Most definitions of loneliness would use feeling words, such as *despair*, *emptiness*, *hopelessness* or *craving for contact*. Other phrases that might define loneliness for some people might include:

- Not having friends;
- Feeling isolated;
- Friendlessness;
- Feeling left out;
- Not having anyone who cares about you;
- Not having a sense of belonging;
- Feeling invisible;
- Feeling cut off from everybody.

A person may feel lonely when:

- There is no one to share thoughts with.
- They have no one to do things with.
- Their need for affection is not met.

Loneliness is not all bad. Some people may see it positively and use periods when they feel lonely to reflect and reassess what they think is important in life. Others may find it helpful to stay with a feeling of 'emptiness' for a period, in preparation for making changes and getting involved again or 'filling up'.

The techniques and strategies used in this session are practical and commonsense ways of controlling and managing shyness, and dealing with loneliness. Many of the other sessions supplied provide a background of skills needed, such as conversational skills, learning to listen and so on. As you go through the exercises you will need to refer to them.

Preparing to do the activities

How shy am I?

Being shy means being nervous or worried about what other people are thinking about you. It may show itself by you avoiding situations or activities where you might become the centre of people's attention. Shyness may apply to particular situations or to a person across situations.

Shyness will affect different people in different ways and in different situations, so consequently what it means to them will differ. Whether individuals feel embarrassed, humiliated, ashamed or whatever, the principal reason for the feelings will be that they are concerned about what other people are thinking about them.

Ensure that everyone understands by the end of the activity that thoughts lead to feelings, physical reactions and the consequential outcome.

Managing shyness

If you are able to extend the activity time, it is helpful to practise as a group using skills such as relaxation, coping self-talk and visualisation outlined in Handout 2. If there is not time, emphasise the need for people to practise these skills at home. Handout 3 enables people to plan what strategy, or combination of strategies, will be most useful in different circumstances. If a strategy is not effective, the plan needs to be reviewed. The usual reason for lack of effectiveness is that the strategy is not being applied realistically or the wrong strategy for that person has been chosen and it needs to be changed.

Who is lonely?

This exercise is very powerful and helps individuals bring to mind what loneliness means to them and how it affects them. Thinking about what life would be like if they did not feel lonely, as well as helping them to identify how they want their life to be, provides a good incentive.

When individuals are feeling negative about their progress or are lacking in motivation, encourage them to repeat this exercise. Once they have been working on the difficulties for a while they can also see how far they have travelled towards their goal.

Relieving loneliness

The suggestions provided are only intended to enable individuals to start thinking about the best ways to meet their own needs. The answer for some may be to concentrate on some of the skills on this course to solve difficulties in relationships already established; others may need to look outwards to form relationships or require a combination of the two. Solutions are very individual. Two people with the same problem may choose different solutions.

Overcoming barriers

Often, loneliness is created by individuals themselves: how they think and behave. This exercise enables people to look at barriers that may be contributing to their loneliness. These barriers can be raised for a variety of reasons, including shyness, lack of assertiveness skills, lack of self-esteem and so on. This is quite a difficult exercise for some people to do, particularly if they lack insight into their own behaviour. It requires honesty and may involve them checking how other people perceive them.

Completing the 'Overcoming barriers' chart (Handout 6) will help to provide motivation as well as to plan how to overcome the barrier.

14 Overcoming shyness and loneliness

Objectives	Activity	Time (in mins)
To remind the group members about what was learnt in the previous session, to give an opportunity to discuss issues or feedback about homework and to set the aims for the current session	**Review the previous session, obtain feedback from homework and set the aim for this session**	10
To examine what shyness is and what effect it has on people	**How shy am I?**	15
To look at strategies to help manage shyness	**Managing shyness**	30
BREAK		10
To become more aware of what loneliness is and its effect on lives	**Who is lonely?**	15
To identify ways of overcoming loneliness	**Relieving loneliness**	15
To plan ways of breaking down barriers to being supported	**Overcoming barriers**	20
To check outcomes have been achieved and to explain the homework assignment	**Review the session and set homework assignment**	5

14 Activity guidelines

Review the previous session, obtain feedback from the homework and state the aims of the current session

Go round the group members and ask them to state something from the previous session that they do well.

How shy am I?

Ask the group members to define shyness and how it affects people. Give out Handout 1 and then, using the headings in Handout 1, ask people to call out what their feelings, thoughts, physical reactions and the outcomes are when they have been experiencing shyness.

Examples might be:

Thoughts	Feelings	Physical reactions
I look silly	anxious	blushing
They think I'm an idiot	lonely	feeling faint
I don't know what to say	embarrassed	heart pounding
I can't talk to him	ashamed	dry mouth
I've no confidence	tense	difficulty breathing
I want out of here	fearful	sweating

Outcome:

- ★ Silence
- ★ Agreeing with everything
- ★ Stammering
- ★ Avoiding people
- ★ Clowning to cover up
- ★ Leaving

Managing shyness

Distribute Handout 2, then go through it and discuss all the strategies outlined. Now give out Handout 3 and explain how to use the chart. First, individuals write down the situation that they find difficult, what their feelings, thoughts and so on are, using the chart. Next, they plan what strategies they can use and what the realistic outcome will be. Lastly, of course, they have to do what is planned.

Who is lonely?

Ask the group members to sit back, close their eyes, relax and think of a time when they felt lonely. Ask them to pay attention to what they were feeling and remain with it for a moment. When time has been allowed for this, ask members to share what loneliness means to them. Write the conclusions up on a white-board or flip-chart.

Once the above has been completed, ask everyone to sit back and relax again. This time ask people to think of how they would like it to be if they were not lonely, or if they can think of a time when they did not feel lonely. When sufficient time has been allowed, ask the group to share what this means to them. Note: being lonely and not being lonely will mean vastly different things to different people.

Relieving loneliness

Ask the group members to call out different ways they can think of to help to overcome loneliness. When suggestions have been exhausted, distribute Handout 4. People can add any ideas not listed there.

Overcoming barriers

Handout 5 lists many of the things that can contribute to people being lonely. Give each group member a copy of the handout and ask them to identify barriers which apply to them. Space is provided for people to add any barriers that are not listed. Handout 6 provides a format for helping individuals to plan to overcome any barriers they have identified. Give the handout to everyone and explain its use.

Homework

Have group members complete Handout 3 for a situation that they find difficult and complete Handout 6 for any barriers to overcoming loneliness that they have identified.

Handout 1 Shyness reaction chart

Situations	Thoughts	Feelings	Physical reaction	Outcomes

Handout 2 Strategies for coping with shyness (1 of 3)

Practise using the following strategies.

Social skills

Develop the skills on this course, in particular:

- Conversational skills: how to open, carry on and close a conversation, having something to say;
- Body language: reading other people's non-verbal communications and responding appropriately, presenting a positive image and using body language to reinforce what you are saying;
- Listening skills: using door-openers to aid interaction, positive voice messages, body language and other active listening skills.

Relaxation skills

Practise using different methods of relaxation. Here are two:

- Rapid relaxation: take a deep breath and exhale slowly. As you breathe out, imagine the tension and stress draining away. Repeat this twice. Do not repeat a third time or you may experience dizziness.
- Using a mental device: if possible, sit down somewhere, close your eyes and imagine something that you find pleasant, relaxing and safe. This could be sitting by a stream, listening to music, smelling or touching something. Imagine the device, focus on it and let calmness take over.

Handout 2 Strategies for coping with shyness (2 of 3)

Coping self-talk

This skill will enable you to remain calm and affirm your ability to cope with the situation, for example:

☆ Negative self-talk: I am going to find this staff meeting very difficult. Everyone's attention will be on me and what I say. I must not make a mistake or everyone will think I'm an idiot. I am really nervous now and when the meeting starts this will get worse.

☆ Coping self-talk: I am feeling nervous, but I can use my relaxation skills to help me relax before the meeting starts. I can use my conversation skills to chat to a few people. When my turn comes to say something to the meeting, I know what I need to say. It doesn't have to be perfect. If anyone doesn't understand anything, I can explain when they ask questions at the end. It will be fine.

Visualisation skills

Visualisation is a very powerful tool to help build confidence, reduce anxiety and help you to feel comfortable in situations. Repeat it as often as you like before any event.

☆ Focus on the situation that you find difficult.
☆ Close your eyes, relax and breathe deeply twice. Let the tension flow away as you breathe out.
☆ Imagine yourself somewhere or doing something that you find peaceful and relaxing. Think about it for a moment and feel yourself relax.
☆ Now, imagine yourself coping with the situation, using the strategies you have chosen and overcoming any fear you have. Think about how it will feel and what it will be like to have achieved what you want.

Handout 2 Strategies for coping with shyness *(3 of 3)*

Replace faulty thinking with realistic thinking

Faulty or unrealistic thinking undermines self-esteem and confidence and raises your anxiety levels. Realistic and supportive thinking helps to motivate and aid you to achieve your goals. Faulty thinking usually falls into the following categories:

- Catastrophising: this is anticipating total disaster if something minor goes wrong. An example is: 'That man is looking at me. I must look a mess'.
- Exaggeration: this is magnifying things beyond the limits of truth. You knock over a drink and then worry for the rest of the party that everyone thinks you are a fumbling idiot.
- Dismissing the positive: you dismiss the positive when you turn positive events into a negative. An example is 'He's only talking to me because he's sorry for me'. You also dismiss the positive when you overlook all your personal strengths and successes, continually ignore achievements and dwell on failures.
- Overgeneralisation: having one bad experience leads you to believe that every experience will be bad.
- Setting impossible standards: this is expecting always to be able to do everything perfectly and never make a mistake. Negative thoughts are prefixed with words like: 'I should cope with …', 'I ought …', 'I must …' These statements are usually followed by thoughts such as 'I'll never be able to do this', 'I can't do it', 'I'm a failure.'
- Making assumptions: this is making assumptions and jumping to conclusions with regard to the facts. Thoughts include: 'Everyone thinks I'm a fool', 'Nobody likes me'.

Handout 3 Shyness action chart

Situation	Thoughts	Feelings	Physical reaction	Anxiety level (0–100)	Outcome

Situation	Strategies I can use	Coping self-talk	Feelings and physical reactions	Anxiety level (0–100)	Outcome

This page may be photocopied for instructional use only. *Positive Interaction Skills* © Robin Dynes 2004

Handout 4 Overcoming loneliness suggestions

- Join a club.
- Enrol for an adult learning class.
- Plan what to do when spending time alone.
- Do something creative.
- Make up your mind to enjoy time alone.
- Get involved in community activity.
- Go to social events.
- Do voluntary work.
- Write letters to friends.
- Chat to a friend on the phone.
- Read a novel.
- Engage in small talk with people you meet in the supermarket, library and other public places.
- Ask someone to join you for lunch, a walk, to go to the cinema or another activity.
- Take exercise – go swimming, go jogging or play a sport such as bowling or golf.
- Recognise your feelings and do something about them.
- Enjoy time alone by using it to listen to music or doing something you enjoy.
- Start thinking positively about being on your own by replacing negative thoughts with positive thoughts ('I hate time alone' could become 'Good, I'm alone tonight, I can listen to my music').
- Think positively about yourself. Substitute thoughts such as 'I'm always on my own. Nobody likes me', with 'I am likeable. I enjoy other people's company and they enjoy being with me. I have lots of good points'.
- Use the skills learnt on this course to make new friends, keep friends and deepen relationships.
- Offer to help others.

Handout 5 Identifying barriers

Barrier	Yes	No
I am continually talking about myself		
I betray confidences		
I seem to be nagging regularly		
I indulge in rude and offensive behaviour		
I am always criticising others		
I don't listen to what other people are saying		
I use bad or offensive language		
I am complaining all the time		
I dramatise everything		
I don't respect other people's boundaries		
I am negative about everything		
I am frightened of being rejected		
I will only do what I want		
I am unreliable		
I make 'racist' comments		
I don't keep in touch with people		
I depend on others contacting me		
I talk incessantly		
I don't support others, but expect them to support me		
I think I am always right		
I make fun of others		
I tell lies		
I have a 'bossy' attitude		
I always know what's best for everyone		
I keep people at a distance		
I don't trust anyone		

Handout 6 Overcoming barriers chart

Behaviour	What I get out of it	What does this cost me?	What I would gain if I did not do this	What I could do instead

Session 14: Overcoming shyness and loneliness

15 Building confidence and self-esteem

Aim

To help group members discover how they feel about themselves and learn how to create positive feelings of confidence and self-worth.

Learning Objectives

By the end of the session group members will understand:

☆ What being 'confident' and having 'self-esteem' means to them;

☆ What they like and dislike about themselves;

☆ Their personal strengths;

☆ How to rebut unrealistic demands they make on themselves;

☆ How to enhance their confidence and self-esteem.

15 Introduction

Having confidence and self-esteem are very important elements in interacting successfully in all situations and forming meaningful relationships. Being confident is really something of a mental attitude – people are as confident as they think they are. The challenge is to reorientate thinking in a more positive way. Life with little or no self-esteem is a very painful business. A person who lacks self-esteem will not be able to have most of their needs met.

A sense of self-worth is formed through awareness of self. The person forms an identity and then attaches a value to themselves. They define who and what they are and make up their mind if they like themself or not.

When a person rejects part of themself as unacceptable, it causes a great deal of pain. This, in turn, causes the person to avoid anything that might stimulate that pain of self-rejection. The person takes fewer risks with friends, socially or at work. It becomes more difficult to meet people, go to social occasions, apply for a job or try for anything that they might not succeed at. There is a lack of ability to be open in interactions, express opinions, give and receive compliments, solve problems, ask for help, socialise and have their needs met. Fears race out of control.

This may include fear of:

- Success, failure or change;
- Making mistakes;
- Being unable to cope;
- Not being loveable;
- Lack of physical attraction;
- Intimacy;
- Exposing the inner self;
- Being hurt or hurting emotionally.

In order to protect themself, the person becomes defensive. This may express itself with anger, bragging, telling lies, making excuses or in the use of alcohol or drugs as a way of coping or escaping.

This session looks at strategies for stopping people making these sorts of judgements and helps them to change their perceptions and feelings about themselves.

Preparing to do the activities

Defining confidence and self-esteem

What makes group members feel 'confident' and their individual ideas about what having 'self-esteem' means will vary. Some will focus on values, others on feelings, cognitive or behavioural aspects. This will help you to encompass all the different factors involved.

Thinking about me

Group members sometimes have difficulty thinking of and acknowledging what they like about themselves. If this happens, they can be prompted by the other person when they are paired up. That person can make suggestions such as 'I think you have a good sense of humour, don't you like that?'

Messages

As with most of the exercises, and to make yourself aware of the difficulties of doing this exercise, think about some of the messages you have received from your own parents and others and how these have formed the rules and demands you make on yourself. Being able to rebut and replace faulty thinking with more realistic and enabling statements is essential to avoid undermining confidence and self-esteem.

Building confidence and self-esteem

You will be able to refer to other sessions for more details on some of the strategies outlined for helping to build confidence and self-esteem, such as assertiveness. It is helpful for group members to be aware of how all the various skills link into their personal development. This will help to motivate and encourage them to revisit previous session information and continue to practise and build on all the skills needed to assist them to develop.

15 Building confidence and self-esteem

Objectives	Activity	Time (in mins)
To remind the group members about what was learnt from the previous session, to give an opportunity to discuss issues or feedback about homework and to set the aims for the current session	**Review the previous session, obtain feedback from homework and set the aim for this session**	10
To look at perceptions of confidence and self-esteem	**Defining 'confidence' and 'self-esteem'**	10
To enable individuals to discover their own strengths	**Thinking about me**	30
BREAK		10
To help individuals recognise their own unrealistic beliefs	**Messages**	30
To explore ways of enhancing confidence and self-esteem	**Building 'confidence' and 'self-esteem'**	25
To check outcomes have been achieved and to explain the homework assignment	**Review the session and set homework assignment**	5

15 Activity guidelines

Review the previous session, obtain feedback from the homework and state the aims of the current session

Go round the group members and ask them to state something from the previous session that they do least well and are working to improve.

Defining confidence and self-esteem

Have a discussion about what having 'confidence' and 'self-esteem' means to group members. Handout 1, which you can use to prompt ideas for discussion, can be given out at the end of the activity.

Positive Interaction Skills

Thinking about me

Ask the group members to call out strengths individuals might have and write a selection of these up on a board. Give out Handout 2 and ask them, individually, to complete what they like and dislike about themselves. When the group members have completed this, divide them into pairs and ask the pairs to help each other with suggestions about how they can turn dislikes into likes and what needs to be changed to achieve this. During the last five minutes of this activity, ask individuals to write positive descriptions of themselves. Alternatively, or if there is time, have each person share their positive description with the whole group.

Messages

Everyone gets messages about themselves from the people around them. These include parents, relatives, friends, colleagues, teachers and others with whom they come into contact. These messages may be direct or indirect, through attitude and so on. The most powerful are those we receive when we are growing up. These messages are interpreted into rules that people live by, such as 'I am not important', 'I'm OK', 'I'm clever', or 'I must never make mistakes'. When people focus on negative messages and interpret them in an unrealistic way, they form a negative image of themselves, resulting in a lack of confidence and self-esteem and destructive self-talk. Explain this and discuss with the group:

> ☆ What are the messages?
> ☆ Are they always true?

After the discussion, distribute Handout 3 and ask the group members to write down unrealistic rules that they have formed about themselves from the messages they have received. When this activity is completed, divide the group members into pairs and have them work together to form rebuttal or realistic self-talk statements for the unrealistic rules.

Building confidence and self-esteem

Distribute Handout 4. Go through it and discuss the ideas for improving confidence and self-esteem. Encourage individuals to generate as many examples as possible from each suggestion.

Homework

Give out Handout 5, ask everyone to rate their skills in building confidence and self-esteem, identify areas they need to work on and plan how they will do this.

Handout 1 Defining confidence and self-esteem

Being 'confident' and having 'self-esteem' means:

- Feeling equal to others;
- Liking and respecting myself;
- Feeling competent;
- Having a sense of being accepted;
- Feeling good about myself;
- Being able to interact positively with others;
- Accepting myself;
- Being accountable and responsible for myself;
- Understanding my personal strengths and weaknesses and knowing I am able to change;
- Being able to appreciate my own worth;
- Being able to accept who I am;
- Having the ability to pursue and achieve my goals;
- Being able to relate equally with others;
- Concentrating on what I want for myself, rather than competing with others all the time;
- Being able to appreciate the worth of other people;
- Having the ability to solve problems.

Handout 2 Likes and dislikes

What I like about myself:	What I dislike about myself:

Ways I can change what I 'dislike' into 'likes'

My positive description of myself is:

15 Handout 3 Messages

Faulty thinking rules I have formed	Realistic (rebuttal) self-talk

Handout 4 Building confidence and self-esteem (1 of 3)

Accept and give compliments

Accept and acknowledge compliments. If someone says you have done something well, thank them and acknowledge it to yourself. In your own mind tell yourself: 'Yes, I did do a good job'. If someone does something for you, show your appreciation by paying them a compliment.

Express your feelings and needs

Your needs and feelings are just as important as those of other people. Not expressing them will reinforce feelings of being less worthy and deserving. Keep aware of your feelings and thoughts and express them.

Accept yourself

Be aware of your likes and dislikes about yourself. Change your dislikes where possible. Accept that you are good at some things and not so good at others. Do not compare yourself with other people. What they want from life will be very different from your own vision.

Set realistic goals

Be realistic about what you can and cannot do. Set goals which are attainable. Avoid trying to live up to other people's expectations – goals must be your own, what you want.

Turn faulty thinking into realistic thinking

(See Session 14: Handout 2.) Avoid catastrophising, exaggeration, dismissing the positive, overgeneraliations, setting impossible standards or making assumptions. Add to this:

- ☆ Mind reading: that is, assuming you know what other people are thinking. They are not always thinking the worst.
- ☆ Filtering: paying attention only to negative stimuli (loss, rejection, unfairness) and rejecting the positive.

Handout 4 Building confidence and self-esteem (2 of 3)

- ☆ Always blaming yourself: even if it is something not under your control. This blinds you to your good qualities.
- ☆ Emotional reasoning: everyone has sad, joyful, boring or exciting days. If you *feel* useless because of your mood it does not mean you *are* useless. Feeling unworthy does not mean you are unworthy. Correct your negative self-talk with realistic self-talk.
- ☆ Challenge self-criticisms: self-criticism often asks you to be perfect, to be prepared for the worst, compare yourself with others, impose rules made by others or live up to other people's expectations. Challenge your self-criticisms and replace them with realistic self-talk.

Take care of yourself

Learn to appreciate your body and take care of it. Eat a sensible diet and take exercise. Equally, appreciate your mind, exercise it and learn to think realistically and positively. Challenge thinking that undermines your abilities.

Learn to be forgiving

This applies both to yourself and others. Avoid being overly critical, either of yourself or others, and do not allow resentments to grow. Everyone makes mistakes and this is how people learn and develop.

Take risks and make changes

Try new things. Change is always frightening even when it brings changes that you want.

Appreciate your own qualities

Focus on your own abilities and qualities, take stock and acknowledge them.

Handout 4 Building confidence and self-esteem *(3 of 3)*

Use visualisation skills

Use visualisation skills to imagine yourself taking a planned risk and succeeding. Ask yourself what your behaviour would be if you felt confident and had good self-esteem. Create an image of yourself feeling good about your abilities. See and hear yourself giving and receiving compliments, completing tasks, saying what you feel and think.

Use affirmations

Affirmations are strong, positive statements ('I am confident', 'I am OK', 'I am likeable', 'I am a good friend', 'I did a good job'). Use these liberally; they are especially powerful when used at the end of visualising yourself doing something.

Use assertiveness skills

These skills are very important in helping you to feel confident and building your self-esteem.

Handout 5 Confidence and self-esteem checklist

Rate your confidence and self-esteem in the following areas:

Rate your abilities in the following areas:	Poor				Good
I accept and give compliments	1	2	3	4	5
I express my feelings, thoughts and needs	1	2	3	4	5
I accept myself	1	2	3	4	5
I set realistic goals	1	2	3	4	5
I turn faulty thinking into realistic thinking	1	2	3	4	5
I take care of myself both mentally and physically	1	2	3	4	5
I am forgiving to myself and others	1	2	3	4	5
I take risks and make changes	1	2	3	4	5
I appreciate my own qualities	1	2	3	4	5
I use visualisation skills	1	2	3	4	5
I use affirmations	1	2	3	4	5
I use my assertiveness skills	1	2	3	4	5

The areas I can improve are:

I will do this by:

16 Managing emotions

Aim
To enable group members to become aware of their emotions, respond to them and learn strategies to manage them.

Learning Objectives
By the end of the session group members will understand:

- The emotions they are experiencing;
- How they respond to them;
- The effects they have;
- Strategies to manage them better.

Introduction

Emotions are experienced continuously while interacting within relationships. In order to have a satisfactory relationship, a person needs to be able to express and manage their emotions and feelings. What a person thinks influences what they feel and how they act. There is a continuous reaction between thoughts, feelings and actions.

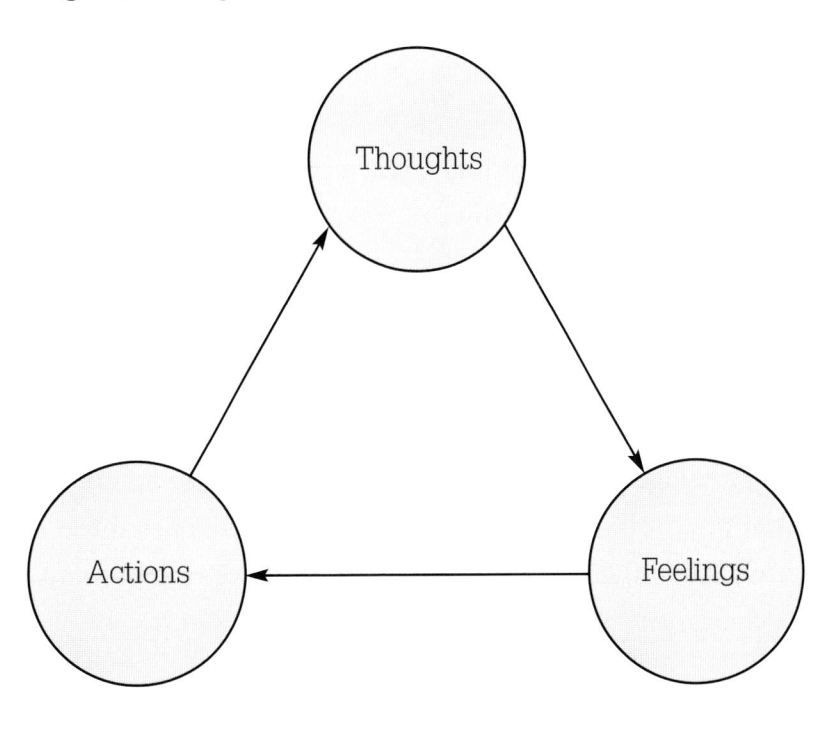

This session is intended to enable individuals to recognise their own emotions and be able to manage their own feelings and responses.

An example of this might be that a woman is having a conversation with a neighbour in the front garden when looking after her young son. Suddenly she hears the sound of tyres screeching. Heart pounding, she runs out to the road to see that a car has just stopped in time before hitting her son who has run out in front of it. She is upset, angry and feels guilty for allowing herself to become so absorbed in the conversation and leaving the gate open. She determines that she will not allow herself to be distracted in this way again. She acknowledges her feelings, accepts responsibility, evaluates the situation and works out what to do in the future to avoid the same thing happening again.

Emotions can be managed in a positive or negative way. The activities in the session provide a forum to discuss this, a method of examining personal reactions to emotions and strategies to manage them in a helpful way.

Preparing to do the activities

Understanding your emotions

Whilst writing emotions and feelings on a flip-chart, ask the group members what relationship interactions might be like without emotions and feelings. Also ask what having emotions and feelings brings to interactions with others.

When preparing for the session, think about an emotional experience that you have had similar to that described in Handout 1. Did it have a negative outcome? How else could it have been managed to provide a more useful outcome? If the experience has a positive outcome, can you imagine how it could have been negative?

Group members may also be able to give examples of their own.

Reactions

Point out to the group that thinking through and discussing experiences of past emotions can sometimes be painful. The activity provides what may be the first opportunity for some people to discuss these issues. Make it clear that if anyone becomes upset or feels they do not want to share their experiences with others, they do not have to do so.

Managing your emotions

Many of the skills learnt in other sessions should be present in the suggestions the group members offer for this activity. Also, many of the same strategies should appear under different emotional headings. Handout 3 is not intended as a definitive list of strategies. It merely demonstrates the type of suggestions expected.

As a group facilitator it will be helpful for you to have completed these exercises in relation to emotions and feelings that you have had difficulty managing.

16 Managing emotions

Objectives	Activity	Time (in mins)
To remind the group members about what was learnt in the previous session, to give an opportunity to discuss issues or feedback about homework and to set the aims for the current session	Review the previous session, obtain feedback from homework and set the aim for this session	10
To enable group members to become aware of the emotions they experience	Understanding your emotions	20
To examine how each person reacts to different emotions	Reactions	30
BREAK		10
To explore strategies for managing emotions	Managing your emotions	45
To check outcomes have been achieved and to explain the homework assignment	Review the session and set homework assignment	5

16 Activity guidelines

Review the previous session, obtain feedback from the homework and state the aims of the current session

Ask the group members to call out learning points they remember from the previous session.

Understanding your emotions

Ask the group members to call out different emotions and feelings, and write them up on a flip-chart or white-board. These might include:

happiness	love	guilt	sadness
anticipation	anger	fear	optimism
shame	disappointment	pride	jealousy

Positive Interaction Skills

Now ask the group members to divide these into negative and positive emotions. Ask them if they think an emotion by itself can be negative or positive, or does this depend on the situation and how the emotion is managed?

Explain to the group that a person is faced with a situation, which sparks an emotion that is fuelled by thoughts and a physical reaction resulting in an outcome. Whether or not that outcome is negative or positive depends on how the emotion is managed. Give out Handout 1, which gives an example of both a negative and positive outcome from a situation. Discuss.

Reactions

Distribute Handout 2 and ask the group members to write down situations for each emotion listed that they have experienced, what their thoughts, physical reaction and the outcome was in each case. When complete, ask them to share some of their findings with the group. What emotions did individuals manage well and what emotions did they find difficult?

Managing your emotions

Divide the group members into three subgroups. Give each group two of the following emotions and ask them to come up with a list of strategies for handling the emotions.

| anger | fear/anxiety | sadness |
| disappointment | shame | guilt |

When this activity has been completed, get everyone back together and have each group share their findings. Handout 3 can be given out and any strategies listed on it that have not appeared can be discussed.

Complete the exercise by giving out Handout 4 and asking individuals to complete it for any of the emotions listed in Handout 2 that presented any difficulties. This time the group members can insert strategies they can use and chart a managed outcome.

Homework

Distribute Handout 5, ask everyone to rate their ability to manage their emotions, identify areas to work on and plan how they will do this.

Handout 1 Reaction chain

Negative management of feelings

Situation	Feelings	Thoughts	Physical reaction	Outcome
Went for an interview for promotion and was turned down	Disappointed	That was awful. Got a lot of the questions wrong. I'm hopeless. Everyone will think I'm an idiot.	Dropped and hunched shoulders. Feel flushed. Drained of energy. Want to hide away.	'I'm not applying again. They know I'm useless.'

Positive management of feelings

Situation	Feelings	Thoughts	Physical reaction	Outcome
Went for an interview for promotion and was turned down	Disappointment	That was hard. I lost my way on some of the questions but did well on some others. I need to do more research so I can do better next time.	A bit tired, but satisfied I did my best on this occasion.	'Pleased I had a go. I can learn from my mistakes and get it right next time an opportunity comes up.'

226 Positive Interaction Skills

Handout 2: Emotional reaction chains experienced

Situations	Feelings	Thoughts	Physical reaction	Outcomes
	Anger			
	Guilt			
	Fear/anxiety			
	Disappointment			
	Shame			
	Sadness			

Session 16: Managing emotions

Handout 3 Strategies for managing feelings (1 of 3)

Managing anger

- Express feelings and fears;
- Make an effort to see other viewpoints;
- Be aware of the harm anger and violence can do;
- Improve communication skills;
- Challenge irrational beliefs;
- Take responsibility for your own feelings and do not blame the other person;
- Use assertiveness skills;
- Learn to manage conflicts;
- Maintain good relationships;
- Find constructive ways to channel anger energy;
- Build better self-esteem to overcome fears of inadequacy;
- Use diversions – games or activities you like to do. Find what works for you and use it to help keep you calm;
- Reduce frustrations in your life;
- Avoid drugs and alcohol as a way of dealing with problems.

Managing anxiety or fear

- Practise breathing exercises;
- Use calming self-talk;
- Use diversions – fantasies, picture pleasant scenes, imagine a favourite piece of music;
- Challenge faulty thinking;
- Use relaxation techniques;
- Release tension through exercise and activity;
- Use visualisation techniques;
- Use problem-solving skills;
- Confront the fear.

Disappointment

- Find a different way to look at the situation;
- Review your goal – was it too ambitious? Should you have prepared better?
- Use diversion techniques;

Handout 3 Strategies for managing feelings (2 of 3)

- Learn what works for you from experience;
- Plan small but regular treats;
- Express your disappointment;
- Check what other people feel – are you being reasonable?
- Use coping self-talk.

Shame

- Avoid what makes your self-dislike worse;
- Focus on distractions;
- Let go of your self-dislike;
- Remind yourself about your good points;
- Use visualisation techniques to dissipate shame;
- Use your self-nurturing voice ('It's OK to look after myself');
- Replace shaming self-talk with positive self-talk ('I deserve respect');
- Forgive yourself for your shortfalls;
- Acknowledge your feeling, express it and move on;
- Stop shaming and blaming;
- Stop being hard on yourself;
- Look at the sources of your shame;
- Do something positive when you feel bad – things that give you a sense of well-being or help you relax;
- Communicate with other people;
- Don't compare yourself with other people.

Guilt

- Forgive yourself and move on;
- Own up to your own guilt and take responsibility for it;
- Challenge if the guilt is reasonable – is the feeling out of proportion to the crime?
- If it is possible to make reparation for the crime do so and move on;
- If possible, acknowledge and share what has happened;
- Challenge if the guilt has been imposed by another person ('If you really cared about me you would …');
- Use diversion techniques when feeling bad;
- Avoid isolation, drugs, alcohol;

Handout 3 Strategies for managing feelings (3 of 3)

- ☆ Challenge the 'shoulds' ('I should be able to …') and other perfectionist notions;
- ☆ Make a commitment to being honest;
- ☆ Accept the guilt;
- ☆ Appreciate your strengths;
- ☆ Identify the type of guilt: religious, values, thought, social, survivor, or an actual crime;
- ☆ Accept that 'life matters and everyone is worth something'.

Sadness

- ☆ Use coping self-talk;
- ☆ Acknowledge the depression;
- ☆ Stay with it if something has happened. It is OK to be sad for a while;
- ☆ Avoid isolation;
- ☆ Express feelings, talk about it;
- ☆ Take regular exercise;
- ☆ Seek counselling if prolonged or unduly intense;
- ☆ Write down your feelings;
- ☆ Get involved in activities with other people.

Handout 4 Coping strategies for emotional reaction chains

Situations	Feelings	Strategies I can use	Thoughts	Physical reaction	Outcomes

Handout 5 Managing emotions checklist

Rate your ability to handle the emotions listed and add three other emotions or feelings not listed which you would like to manage more effectively.

Rate your abilities in the following areas:	Poor				Good
Anger	1	2	3	4	5
Fear or anxiety	1	2	3	4	5
Disappointment	1	2	3	4	5
Shame	1	2	3	4	5
Guilt	1	2	3	4	5
Sadness	1	2	3	4	5
Happiness	1	2	3	4	5
	1	2	3	4	5
	1	2	3	4	5
	1	2	3	4	5

The emotions I can learn to manage better are:

I will do this by:

17 Improving self-management skills

Aim

To raise group members' awareness of the impact self-management skills can have on interactions and relationships, and to plan to improve on them.

Learning Objectives

By the end of the session group members will understand:

- ☆ The importance of managing themselves and their relationships;
- ☆ The links between self-management and enjoying good relationships;
- ☆ Strategies to improve self-management;
- ☆ How to apply strategies to different situations;
- ☆ How to handle stress or pressure;
- ☆ How to create the right impression.

17 Introduction

This session is intended to help learners to begin to develop the skills to improve their ability to manage themselves, their relationships, stress, the impression they make on others and how people respond to them.

Once individuals are aware of how interactions and responses to them are shaped by their own behaviour, they can begin to manage this to encourage positive responses. Developing self-management skills will enable them to have more control over interactions.

Preparing to do the activities

Self-management and interactions

It is worth looking at what influence self-management has had in the different areas of your own life, such as family, work, socially, with friends and when dealing with authority. How has it influenced your interactions? What has the effect been when you have been effective with your self-management? What has been the effect when you have neglected self-management?

Developing self-management skills entails learning from experience and being appropriate to the situation. Strict time-keeping may be necessary at work, and when dealing with authority, but it may be less important with some family members. A person may take and deal well with criticism at work but deal with it badly at home or with friends in personal relationships.

Strategies

It is important that group members become aware that being able to work out strategies suitable to the situation is more important than the number of strategies they know about. Many strategies have been discussed throughout the course which can be used as part of self-management. Only some are listed in the handout provided.

Handling stress or pressure

A certain amount of stress is necessary to function well. It helps people to reach their peak efficiency. However, if the pressure becomes too much, then performance suffers and things do not go so well. Much can be done to relieve stress and most of its undesirable effects can be prevented by good self-management. This activity presents a simple process to enable individuals to plan the management of their stress. Trying it out using a situation you find stressful will help to build your confidence both in using and presenting it to others.

Creating the right impression

Imagine that you are starting work in a new office. As you are shown around and introduced to people, you begin taking in details about the people you are going to work with. They may say little or nothing at all, but you will begin making assumptions about their abilities, intelligence, character and attitudes, which will affect how you will interact with them. They will also be making similar judgements about you.

Because you are seeing other people, it is difficult to be aware of how rapidly your appearance, what you say and how you say it, body language and attitude make an impression and how lasting that impression can be.

Think about an interview you have conducted. How quickly did you make your mind up about the person and how much was influenced by the impression they created? Think about a recent experience you had meeting new people. How quickly did you make a judgement on impression? What judgements might they have made about you? How did that affect how they responded to you?

Being aware of how important impressions are, how they can affect interactions, and being able to be appropriate is critical when managing how other people respond in a positive way.

17 Improving self-management skills

Objectives	Activity	Time (in mins)
To remind the group members about what was learnt in the previous session, to give opportunity to discuss issues or feedback about homework and to set the aims for the current session	Review the previous session, obtain feedback from homework and set the aims for this session	10
To examine what needs to be managed and how this affects our ability to interact with other people	Self management and interactions	20
To look at a range of strategies that can be used for self-management	Strategies	20
BREAK		10
To develop skills for dealing with stress and pressure	Handling stress or pressure	30
To explore the importance of creating a positive impression and how it affects interactions	Creating the right impression	25
To check outcomes have been achieved and to explain the homework assignment	Review the session and set homework assignment	5

17 Activity guidelines

Review the previous session, obtain feedback from the homework and state the aims of the current session

Ask the group members to state briefly what their week has been like and what they have been able to put into practice from the previous session.

Self-management and interactions

Ask the group members to call out what they need to be able to self-manage. This might include:

- Emotions
- Shyness
- Criticism
- Appearance
- Supportive networks
- Trustworthiness
- Stress or pressure
- Timekeeping
- Conflicts

When the list is completed, or whilst writing the list up on a white-board, ask the group members to expand on the items. How does managing them affect how they interact and get on with other people? End by discussing how managing the issues listed affects interactions in the following areas:

- Family or partners
- Work or career
- Dealing with authority
- Friends or social life

Strategies

Divide the group members into three subgroups. Give each subgroup a sheet of flip-chart paper and a magic marker and ask them to write down as many self-management strategies as they can think of. There are suggestions in Handout 1. End the activity by asking each group to share their suggestions with everyone and distributing the handout.

Handling stress or pressure

Go through the example of managing a situation found stressful in Handout 2. Once completed, distribute Handout 3 and ask the group members to complete their own reaction chart and action plan for an interaction situation that they find stressful. Encourage the group members to use some of the suggestions from the strategies activity as part of their action plans. If there is time available, and group members are comfortable with the idea, have some members share their reaction chart and action plan with the group.

Creating the right impression

Have a discussion with the group about why it is important to create the right impression and how this affects our interactions. Using a flip-chart, write down the ideas put forward by the group. Also, make a list of what happens when the wrong impression is created. Suggestions are provided in Handout 4, which can be distributed when ideas for the flip-chart have been exhausted.

When the activities have been completed, give out Handout 5. Form four subgroups and give each subgroup the task of completing the grids in one of the following situation areas:

- ★ Family
- ★ Work
- ★ Authority
- ★ Friend

Group members should write down what would help to create the right or wrong impressions with use of speech, appearance, body language and attitude. When the activity is complete, have the groups share their conclusions.

Homework

Distribute Handout 6 and ask everyone to rate their self-management skills, identify areas to work on and plan how they will do this.

Handout 1 Strategies

- Break tasks down into manageable steps;
- Set achievable goals;
- Prioritise when under pressure;
- Cultivate new friendships;
- Plan outing with friends;
- Keep a diary to help manage time;
- Be aware of deadlines: what has been promised and when;
- Develop new interests;
- Have a daily plan;
- Spend time with friends;
- Have fun – do things which you enjoy;
- Join in community events;
- Show you are supportive;
- Plan your social life;
- Do a course in personal development;
- Use positive self-talk;
- Release tension through exercise and activity;
- Express your feelings and needs;
- Negotiate compromises.

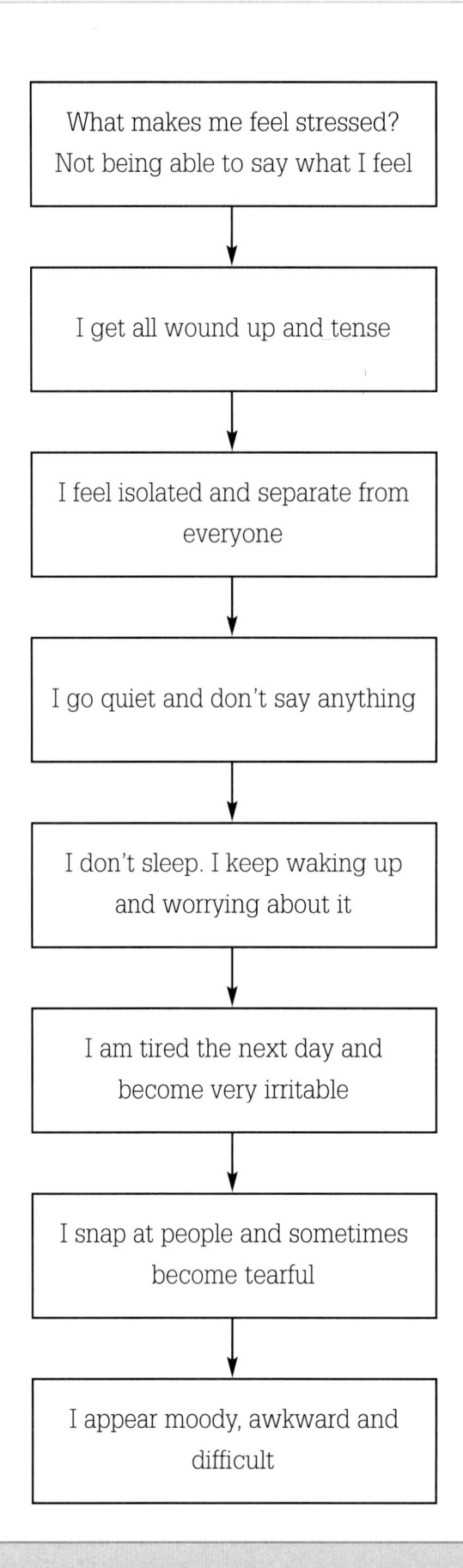

17 Handout 2 Example stress reaction chart and action plan (1 of 2)

```
┌─────────────────────────────────────┐
│  What makes me feel stressed?       │
│  Not being able to say what I feel  │
└─────────────────────────────────────┘
                  ↓
┌─────────────────────────────────────┐
│  I get all wound up and tense       │
└─────────────────────────────────────┘
                  ↓
┌─────────────────────────────────────┐
│  I feel isolated and separate from  │
│  everyone                           │
└─────────────────────────────────────┘
                  ↓
┌─────────────────────────────────────┐
│  I go quiet and don't say anything  │
└─────────────────────────────────────┘
                  ↓
┌─────────────────────────────────────┐
│  I don't sleep. I keep waking up    │
│  and worrying about it              │
└─────────────────────────────────────┘
                  ↓
┌─────────────────────────────────────┐
│  I am tired the next day and        │
│  become very irritable              │
└─────────────────────────────────────┘
                  ↓
┌─────────────────────────────────────┐
│  I snap at people and sometimes     │
│  become tearful                     │
└─────────────────────────────────────┘
                  ↓
┌─────────────────────────────────────┐
│  I appear moody, awkward and        │
│  difficult                          │
└─────────────────────────────────────┘
```

Handout 2 Example stress reaction chart and action plan (2 of 2)

Ideas I can think of to manage the stress and change this are (think of as many ideas as possible):

☆ Think through what I want to say to the person and how I want to say it;
☆ Use positive self-talk;
☆ Distract myself by reading a book;
☆ Do relaxation exercises;
☆ Make an arrangement to see the other person;
☆ Go for a walk before going to bed to make me feel tired;
☆ Imagine myself saying what I need to say.

My action plan is (choose the actions with which you feel comfortable and that will solve the problem):

☆ Think through what I want to say to the person;
☆ Make an arrangement to see the person;
☆ Do relaxation exercises when I feel really stressed and use positive self-talk;
☆ Do relaxation exercises at other times and imagine myself calmly saying what I need to say.

Handout 3 Stress reaction chart and action plan (1 of 2)

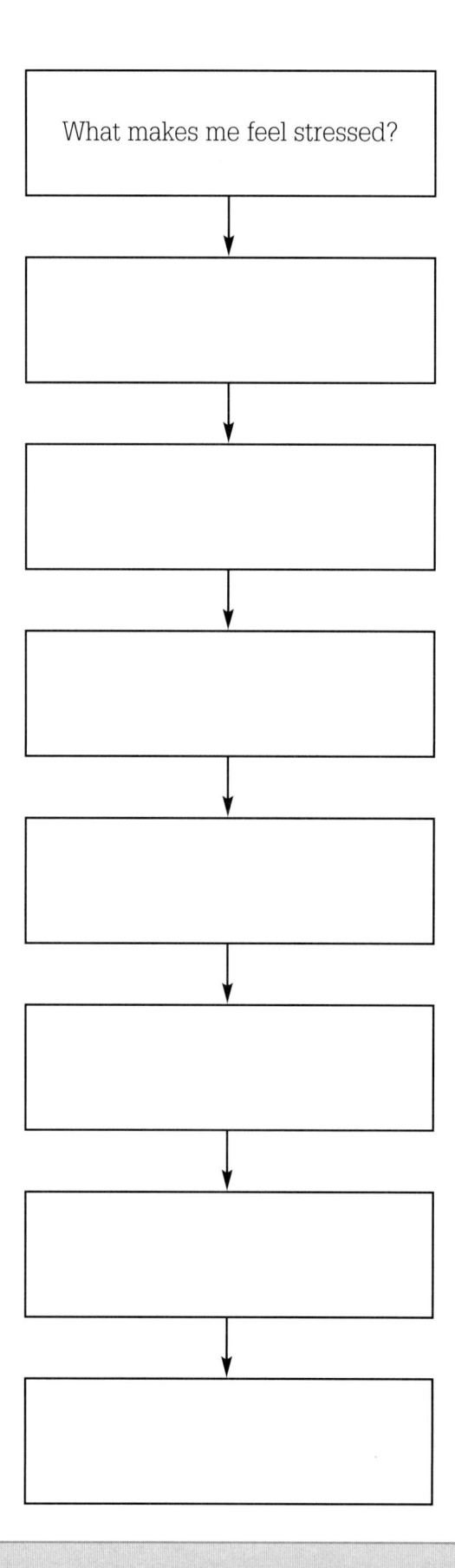

What makes me feel stressed?

Handout 3 Stress reaction chart and action plan (2 of 2)

Ideas I can think of to manage the stress and change this are (think of as many ideas as possible):

My action plan is (choose the actions with which you feel comfortable and that will solve the problem):

Handout 4 Creating the right impression

Reasons for creating the right impression. People will:

☆ React in a more positive way to me;
☆ Want to be involved with me;
☆ Be more likely to help;
☆ Like me;
☆ Find me more attractive;
☆ Cooperate better with me;
☆ Be more likely to ask me to be involved with them.

When the wrong impression is created, people will:

☆ Be more likely to react negatively;
☆ Be less likely to want to be involved with me;
☆ Be less cooperative;
☆ Be less likely to want anything to do with me;
☆ Be more likely to think poorly of me;
☆ Be more likely to think I could be difficult to get along with.

Handout 5 Creating the right impression exercise

Creating the right impression

	Family	Work	Authority	Friend
Speech				
Appearance				
Body language				
Attitude				

Effects of creating the wrong impression

	Family	Work	Authority	Friend
Speech				
Appearance				
Body language				
Attitude				

Handout 6 Self-management checklist

Rate your ability to self-manage in the areas listed.

Rate your abilities in the following areas:	Poor				Good
Managing interactions within the family	1	2	3	4	5
Managing interactions at work	1	2	3	4	5
Dealing with people in authority	1	2	3	4	5
Managing interactions with friends	1	2	3	4	5
Use of strategies	1	2	3	4	5
Handling stress or pressure	1	2	3	4	5
Creating the right impression	1	2	3	4	5

Areas I need to work on are:

I will do this by:

18 Ending the group

Aim

To ensure that group members maintain a positive outlook, review their learning and plan for the future.

Learning Objectives

By the end of the session group members will understand:

☆ How to maintain a positive outlook;

☆ The progress they have made;

☆ What is needed to maintain progress;

☆ An action plan for the future.

Introduction

As this is the last formal session for the group, it is important that an opportunity is provided for group members to review their progress and to ensure they have a plan to continue their development in the future. By the end of the session individual members should be aware of what skills need to be developed further and be clear about how they can go about it.

Everyone should be feeling pleased with their progress on the course. They will also likely be feeling sad that the course is coming to an end. They will need to be reassured that they can continue to make progress on their own. Ensure that there is ample time for farewells at the end of the session. Also, group members may wish to make arrangements for informal meetings in the future.

When preparing for the session, check back on what your own aims and objectives were for the course. Have they been achieved? If not, why not? What has gone well? What has not gone so well? Is there anything you can do in the final session to put things right? What would you do differently the next time you run the course? Have there been some unexpectedly good outcomes?

It is always helpful to ask group members at the end of the previous session to spend some time going through their folders to refresh their memories about what they wanted from the course and what they feel has gone well and not so well.

You might also like give thought to the following:

★ If the group wants to continue to meet in an informal way, who might organise this? Having a list of addresses and telephone numbers of group members would be essential for anyone who volunteers to do this.

★ The group might like to celebrate the end of the course in some way. This could be a pub meal, a barbecue or whatever. Make sure that everyone understands that the final session is a working session and not a celebration!

★ Has there been any unfinished business in any of the sessions? A situation might remain unresolved or something unsaid. Are you aware that there is something someone wants to say, but that an opportunity has not arisen for them to do so?

Preparing to do the activities

A positive outlook

Think through some of the methods that you find useful in maintaining a positive outlook and the situations in which you use them. When do you use positive self-talk? When do you use relaxation techniques? When do you find it helpful to talk something through with a friend?

How far have I come?

You may be able to share some examples of what you have learnt from facilitating the course and your reflections on how you feel the course has progressed to help with discussion in this activity. Some members may feel that, in light of what they have learnt, their original scoring was not a true reflection of their skills at the beginning of the course.

What next?

It will be useful to have drawn up an action plan of your own, using as your goal an area for development that you feel you could strengthen. You can then use this as an example to demonstrate to the group how the action plan should be completed.

Farewell

As a final positive reinforcement it is very effective if you have given some thought to the qualities each student has displayed during the period of the course. You can then end the session by stating a particular strength or quality each learner has shown.

18 Ending the group

Objectives	Activity	Time (in mins)
To remind the group members about what was learnt in the previous session, to give opportunity to discuss issues or feedback about homework and to set the aims for the current session	**Review the previous session, obtain feedback from homework and set the aims for this session**	10
To explore ways of maintaining a positive outlook	**A positive outlook**	20
To review learning and progress made with interaction skills	**How far have I come?**	30
BREAK		10
To enable group members to identify their personal goals for the future	**What next?**	30
To review the session and say goodbye	**Farewell**	20

18 Activity guidelines

Review the previous session, obtain feedback from the homework and state the aims of the current session

Write 'One thing I learned in the last session was …' on a flip-chart and ask each group member to call out a learning point from the previous session and write them up on the chart. Briefly discuss successes and difficulties with the homework and outline the aim for the current session.

A positive outlook

Draw a line down the centre of a flip-chart sheet. Write the headings 'A negative outlook results in:' on one side of the line and 'A positive outlook results in:' on the other. Now have group members brainstorm each heading.

When this activity is complete, put up a new sheet and ask individuals to suggest ideas to prevent a negative outlook and promote a positive outlook. Finish by giving out Handout 1 and asking people to identify methods that might work well for them.

How far have I come?

Distribute Handout 2 and ask individuals to rate their abilities in the areas listed. When everyone has finished the task, give out Handout 2 from Session 1, which everyone originally completed, and ask the group to compare how they rated themselves then with now. Has there been movement in any areas? What do individuals feel that they have learnt? What areas do they need to strengthen? Do they feel that the original aims for the course (ensure that the original flip-chart sheet completed in Session 1 is available) have been achieved? What do they think has gone well and what not so well?

Finish the activity with each person making a statement about something that has changed for them since the course started. It could be phrased: 'At the beginning of the course I ... and now I ...'

What next?

Discuss with the group members how they can maintain and develop their skills in the future. There are some suggestions in Handout 3, which can be distributed after the discussion has been exhausted.

When the topic has been aired sufficiently, give out Handout 4 and ask each person to choose one of the areas they have identified as needing working on from Handout 2 and, using that as a goal, work out an action plan to achieve that goal.

Review and farewell

Check that the aims and outcomes for this session have been achieved. Next, thank everyone for the contribution they have made to the group and ask each person to say something they have learnt from the person on their right or something positive that that person has contributed to the group. Examples might be: 'Ian, you have cheered us up when everyone was feeling low', or 'Shirley, you have been really creative with some of your suggestions'.

Finish the session by reminding people that:

> * They have now been able to evaluate the course and what they have learnt.
> * They have reviewed the areas that they need to work on in the future to maintain and develop their interaction skills, and they have some practical ideas and an action plan to help them to do this.

Handout 1 A positive outlook

Maintaining a positive outlook is essential for improving self-esteem, confidence, maintaining interaction skills and continuing to build on what has been achieved. It is important to respond to situations in a positive way without undermining yourself. A negative outlook results in:

lack of energy	thinking badly about your abilities
low self-esteem	not wanting to interact with others
feeling unworthy	feeling unable to cope
avoiding other people	not enjoying interactions
feeling isolated	thinking badly about others

A positive attitude results in:

feeling energetic	enjoying interacting with others
feeling good	better relationships
taking interest in others	feeling other people care
better self-esteem	looking forward to events
feeling confident	being successful

What can you do to prevent forming a negative outlook and to promote a positive attitude? You can:

☆ Challenge negative thinking;
☆ Use visualisation to see yourself succeeding;
☆ Use positive self-talk;
☆ Set achievable goals;
☆ Manage pressure and stress;
☆ Maintain good, supportive social networks;
☆ Share successes with friends;
☆ Look after your health;
☆ See mistakes as learning opportunities;
☆ Congratulate yourself on achievements, no matter how small;
☆ Build on skills;
☆ Manage criticism in a positive way.

You will be able to identify many more ways that help develop, reinforce and maintain a positive outlook and keep you motivated to build on the work you have begun. Identify particular methods that work well for you and use them regularly.

Handout 2 Skills evaluation checklist

Rate your abilities in the following areas.

Rate your abilities in the following areas:	Poor				Good
Recognising influences on interaction	1	2	3	4	5
Developing supportive social networks	1	2	3	4	5
Understanding body language	1	2	3	4	5
Making conversation	1	2	3	4	5
Listening to others	1	2	3	4	5
Starting, sustaining and ending relationships	1	2	3	4	5
Appreciating other points of view	1	2	3	4	5
Creating trust and learning to self-disclose	1	2	3	4	5
Resolving conflict in relationships	1	2	3	4	5
Being assertive and handling criticism	1	2	3	4	5
Overcoming shyness and loneliness	1	2	3	4	5
Building confidence and self-esteem	1	2	3	4	5
Managing emotions	1	2	3	4	5
Self-management skills	1	2	3	4	5

My strengths are:

Areas I need to strengthen and improve are:

Handout 3 Maintaining and developing skills

Skills can be maintained and developed by:

- Regular practice;
- Developing support networks;
- Keeping the handouts and reading through them;
- Continually reminding yourself of their benefits;
- Expecting some difficulties and setbacks;
- Looking after yourself;
- Regularly reviewing your progress and acknowledging it;
- Doing action plans to achieve goals;
- Reading books on the topics covered. Your local library or bookshop may have additional titles or be able to order them for you;
- Getting together as a group or with friends you have made in the group to share difficulties and successes;
- Finding out about, and doing, other courses in personal development. Adult Education or other classes may be available in your area.

Handout 4 Action plan

Using one of the areas that you have identified as needing strengthening or improving, write this down as a goal and fill in the steps you need to achieve that gaol.

My goal is:

The steps I need to take to achieve it are:

Step 1:

Step 2:

Step 3:

Step 4:

Step 5:

Appendix 1 Interaction skills needs assessment

Dear Colleague,

In order to establish what activities will be most useful when planning future courses, we would like your input so that we can better meet your needs and the needs of your clients or students. Below is listed a range of topics that can be covered in an interaction skills group. Please tick the topics you feel would be most useful to your clients.

Topic	Tick here
Recognising influences on interaction	
Developing supportive social networks	
Understanding body language	
Making conversation	
Listening to others	
Starting, sustaining and ending relationships	
Appreciating other points of view	
Creating trust and self-disclosing	
Resolving conflict in relationships	
Being assertive and handling criticism	
Overcoming shyness and loneliness	
Building confidence and self-esteem	
Managing emotions	
Improving self-management skills	

Comments:

Name _____ Date _____

THANK YOU FOR YOUR COOPERATION.

Please return this form to: _____